OPTIMISM
PRESS

UNREASONABLE
HOSPITALITY

UNREASONABLE HOSPITALITY

The Remarkable Power
of Giving People More
Than They Expect

WILL GUIDARA

OPTIMISM PRESS

OPTIMISM
PRESS

Optimism Press
An imprint of Penguin Random House LLC
penguinrandomhouse.com

Most Penguin Random House books are available at a discount when purchased
in quantity for sales promotions or corporate use. Special editions, which include
personalized covers, excerpts, and corporate imprints, can be created when
purchased in large quantities. For more information, please call (212) 572-2232 or
email specialmarkets@penguinrandomhouse.com. Your local bookstore can
also assist with discounted bulk purchases using the Penguin Random House
corporate Business-to-Business program. For assistance in locating a
participating retailer, email B2B@penguinrandomhouse.com.

Library of Congress Cataloging-in-Publication Data

Names: Guidara, Will, author.
Title: Unreasonable hospitality : the remarkable power of giving people
more than they expect / Will Guidara.
Description: New York : Optimism Press, [2022] |
Includes bibliographical references and index. |
Identifiers: LCCN 2022027969 (print) | LCCN 2022027970 (ebook) |
ISBN 9780593418574 (hardcover) | ISBN 9780593418581 (ebook) |
Subjects: LCSH: Customer services. | Hospitality. | Corporate culture. | Management.
Classification: LCC HF5415.5 .G856 2022 (print) | LCC HF5415.5 (ebook) |
DDC 658.8/12—dc23/eng/20220801
LC record available at https://lccn.loc.gov/2022027969
LC ebook record available at https://lccn.loc.gov/2022027970

Printed in the United States of America
15th Printing

BOOK DESIGN BY ELLEN CIPRIANO

To Frank Guidara—my father, my mentor, and my best friend, for always showing me what "right" looks like, and for helping me see how unbelievably fulfilling a life spent pursuing hospitality could be.

And all the people I worked with at Eleven Madison Park, the NoMad, and Make It Nice—everyone who gave so much of themselves to care for others. This book is a testament to all of you.

CONTENTS

A LETTER FROM SIMON SINEK

At Optimism Press, we imagine a world in which the vast majority of people wake up every single morning inspired, feel safe wherever they are, and end the day fulfilled by the work that they do. And the reality is, we are more likely to build this world if we commit to building it together.

But there's a problem. . . .

Over the last few decades, we've drifted apart. We used to do more things together. We attended church and other places of worship. We met up with friends and neighbors and met new people through bowling leagues and at our local rec centers. But these days, church attendance is down dramatically and bowling leagues and rec centers have all but disappeared. Add in the rise of digital communication and increased demand for remote work and we are left feeling lonelier and more apart than at any other time in recent history. Yet our intense desire to feel a sense of belonging remains—it's an innate human need. That's where *Unreasonable Hospitality* comes in.

On its surface, this is a book about a talented entrepreneur who helped transform a middling brasserie in New York City into the best restaurant in the world. However, this book is much bigger and more important than that. It is a book about how to treat people. How to listen. How to be curious. And how to learn to love the feeling of making others feel welcome. It is a book about how to make people feel like they belong.

The greatest restaurants in the world became great by challenging the way we think about food: sourcing, preparation, presentation and, of course, taste. But when Will Guidara set out to make Eleven Madison Park the best restaurant in the world, he had a crazy idea about how to do it: "What would happen if we approached hospitality with the same passion, attention to detail, and rigor that we bring to our food?"

Most people think of hospitality as something they do. Will thinks about service as an act of service—about how his actions make people feel. And he recognized that if he wanted his frontline teams to obsess about how they made their customers feel, he had to obsess about how he made his *employees* feel. The two cannot be separated: great service cannot exist without great leadership.

Will not only transformed a restaurant, but challenged our entire idea of service. The lessons in *Unreasonable Hospitality* have as much relevance to real estate agents and insurance brokers—even government agencies—as they do for people who work in restaurants and hotels. His thoughts on leadership are as applicable to business-to-consumer companies as they are to business-to-business companies. Indeed, any organization would benefit from his thinking.

In this book, Will shows the amazing impact we can have on someone's life when we give them a sense of belonging . . . and, as important, how inspiring it is to work together to give people that feeling. And that's an idea worth sharing.

Be unreasonable and inspire on!
Simon Sinek

UNREASONABLE HOSPITALITY

CHAPTER 1

WELCOME TO THE
HOSPITALITY ECONOMY

At home, we were on top of the world.

Our restaurant, Eleven Madison Park, had recently received four stars from *The New York Times*, and a couple of James Beard Awards, too. But when my chef-partner Daniel Humm and I arrived at the cocktail reception the night before the awards for the 2010 World's 50 Best Restaurants, we understood: this was a whole different ball game.

Imagine every famous chef and restaurateur you've ever heard of milling around, drinking champagne and catching up with friends—and not one of them was talking to us. I'd never felt so much like a freshman at a new high school trying to figure out where to sit in the cafeteria, not even when I *was* a freshman.

It was a huge honor to be invited. The 50 Best awards had begun in 2002, but they'd become immediately meaningful in the industry. First of all, they were decided by a jury of a thousand well-regarded experts from around the world. And nobody had ever considered before how the best restaurants on the planet ranked against one another. By doing so, the awards gave these restaurants a push to become even better when they might have been content to rest on their laurels.

The awards ceremony itself was held at London's Guildhall, so regal and imposing it might as well have been a palace. As Daniel and I sat down, more than a little intimidated, we foolishly tried to gauge where we were going to land on the list based on where we were sitting relative to chefs like Heston Blumenthal of England's Fat Duck, or Thomas Keller of Per Se, both of whom had been in the top ten the year before.

I guessed forty. Daniel, always more optimistic, guessed number thirty-five.

The lights went down, the music played. The emcee for the night was a handsome, debonair Brit. And while I'm sure there were all the usual formalities and introductions and "thank you for comings" before the bomb dropped, in my memory there was little preamble before the man said, "To kick it off, coming in at number fifty, a new entry from New York City: Eleven Madison Park!"

That knocked the wind right out of us. We slumped over and stared at our feet.

Unfortunately, what we couldn't have possibly known (because it was our first year at this event, and because we were the very first restaurant called) is that when they call your name, they're also projecting your image onto a gigantic screen at the front of the auditorium, so that everyone can see you celebrating your win.

Except we weren't celebrating. We were at the very bottom of the list! Mortified to see our dejected faces on the thirty-foot-tall screen, I elbowed Daniel, and the two of us mustered a smile and a wave, but it was too little, too late: an auditorium filled with the most celebrated chefs and restaurateurs in the world—our heroes—had already borne witness to our devastation. The night was over for us before it had even begun.

At the reception afterward, we ran into Massimo Bottura, the Italian chef of Osteria Francescana, a Michelin three-star based in Modena— and number six on the list (not that we were counting). He saw us, started laughing, and couldn't stop: "You guys looked pretty happy up there!"

Fair enough, but Daniel and I weren't laughing. It was an honor to be recognized as one of the fifty best restaurants in the world; we knew that. Still—in that room, we had come in last place.

We left the party early and headed back to our hotel, where we grabbed a bottle of bourbon from the bar and sat, ready to drown our sorrows, on the steps outside.

We spent the next couple of hours moving through the five stages of grief. We'd staggered out of the auditorium in denial—had that really happened? Then we got mad—who the hell did they think they were? We breezed through bargaining and spent the better part of the bottle on depression before settling into a state of acceptance.

On one level, it's absolutely ridiculous to call any restaurant "the best restaurant in the world." But the importance of the 50 Best list is that it names the places that are having the greatest impact on the world of food at a given moment in time.

The techniques that Spanish chef Ferran Adrià pioneered at El Bulli introduced molecular gastronomy to the world. René Redzepi championed foraged and wild-caught foods from the land and water surrounding his Copenhagen restaurant Noma, and a local food movement was born. And if you've eaten out or walked down the aisles of your local grocery in the last ten years, you've felt the impact those innovations have had on my industry and beyond.

These chefs had the courage to make something no one had made before, and to introduce elements that changed the game for everyone.

We hadn't done that yet. We'd worked our butts off to earn a spot on that list, but what, really, had we done that was groundbreaking? The more we talked, the more it became clear: nothing.

We had everything we needed: the work ethic, the experience, the talent, the team. But we'd been operating as glorified curators, picking the best features of all the great restaurants that had come before us and making them our own.

Our restaurant was excellent and made a lot of people happy. But it hadn't yet changed the conversation.

When I was young, my dad gave me a paperweight that read, "What would you attempt to do if you knew you could not fail?" That's what I was thinking about when Daniel and I wrote, "We will be Number One in the world," on a cocktail napkin.

It was very late, and the bottle was mostly empty by the time we stumbled back to our respective rooms. I was exhausted, but my mind kept racing back to that napkin.

Most of the chefs on the 50 Best list had made their impact by focusing on innovation, on what needed to change. But as I thought about the impact I wanted to make, I focused on the one thing that wouldn't. Fads fade and cycle, but **the human desire to be taken care of never goes away.**

Daniel's food was extraordinary; he was undeniably one of the best chefs in the world. So if we could become a restaurant focused passionately, intentionally, wholeheartedly on connection and graciousness—on giving both the people on our team and the people we served a sense of belonging—then we'd have a real shot at greatness.

I wanted to be number one, but that desire wasn't just about the award; I wanted to be part of the team that made *that* impact.

Just before I drifted off to sleep, I smoothed out the napkin and added two more words:

"Unreasonable Hospitality."

Service Is Black and White; Hospitality Is Color

When I was younger, I took a lot of pride in coming up with interview questions.

I now believe the best interview technique is no technique at all: you simply have enough of a conversation that you can get to know the person a little bit. Do they seem curious and passionate about what we're trying to build? Do they have integrity; are they someone I can respect? Is this someone I can imagine myself—and my team—happily spending a lot of time with?

But before I had the experience to let the conversation flow, one of my favorite questions to ask was, "What's the difference between service and hospitality?"

The best answer I ever got came from a woman I ended up *not* hiring. She said, "Service is black and white; hospitality is color."

"Black and white" means you're doing your job with competence and efficiency; "color" means you make people feel great about the job you're doing for them. Getting the right plate to the right person at the right table is service. But genuinely engaging with the person you're serving, so you can make an authentic connection—that's hospitality.

Daniel Humm and I spent eleven years turning Eleven Madison Park, a beloved but middling two-star brasserie serving seafood towers and soufflés, into the number one restaurant in the world. We got on that 50 Best list by pursuing excellence, the black and white, attending to every detail and getting as close to perfection as we could. But we got to number one by going Technicolor—by offering hospitality so bespoke, so over the top, it can be described only as unreasonable.

We had a radical idea of what the guest experience could be, and our vision was unlike any other out there. "You're not being realistic," someone would invariably tell us, every time we contemplated one of our reinventions. "You're being unreasonable."

That word "unreasonable" was meant to shut us down—to end the conversation, as it so often does. Instead, it started one, and became our call to arms. Because no one who ever changed the game did so by being reasonable. Serena Williams. Walt Disney. Steve Jobs. Martin Scorsese.

Prince. Look across every discipline, in every arena—sports, entertainment, design, technology, finance—you need to be unreasonable to see a world that doesn't yet exist.

Chefs at the finest restaurants in the world had long been celebrated for being unreasonable about the food they served. At Eleven Madison Park, we came to realize the remarkable power of being unreasonable about how we made people feel. I'm writing this book because I believe it's time for every one of us to start being unreasonable about hospitality.

Of course, I hope everyone in my own industry reads this book and makes that choice, but I believe this idea can result in a seismic shift if it extends *beyond* restaurants. For most of this country's history, America functioned as a manufacturing economy; now, we're a service economy, and dramatically so—more than three-quarters of our GDP comes from service industries. So whether you're in retail, finance, real estate, education, health care, computer services, transportation, or communications, you have an incredible opportunity to be just as intentional and creative— as unreasonable—about pursuing hospitality as you are about every other aspect of your business. Because whether a company has made the choice to put their team and their customers at the center of every decision will be what separates the great ones from the pack.

Unfortunately, these skills have never been less valued than they are in our current hyperrational, hyperefficient work culture. We are in the middle of a digital transformation. That transformation has enhanced many aspects of our lives, but too many companies have left the human behind. They've been so focused on products, they've forgotten about people. And while it may be impossible to quantify in financial terms the impact of making someone feel good, don't think for a second that it doesn't matter. In fact, it matters more.

The answer is simple, if not easy: create a culture of hospitality. Which means addressing questions I've spent my career asking: How do you make the people who work for you and the people you serve feel seen and valued? How do you give them a sense of belonging? How do you make them feel part of something bigger than themselves? How do you make them feel welcome?

There's a long-standing debate in my profession as to whether hospitality can be taught. Many leaders I respect believe it can't; I couldn't disagree more. In fact, in 2014, I founded a conference for dining room professionals with my friend Anthony Rudolf, who was at the time the general manager of Per Se, with the intention of doing just that.

Chefs gathered at different conferences around the world, but there wasn't a single one for the people who worked in the dining room. So we set out to create a space where like-minded, passionate people could form community, trade ideas, and inspire one another—and, in so doing, evolve our craft.

We called it the Welcome Conference, and it was an instant hit with restaurant people. Dining room professionals from all over the country attended lectures, networked over drinks, and went home reinvigorated.

By the conference's third year, though, when we looked out into the audience, we saw sommeliers and servers sitting next to people who didn't work in restaurants at all: tech titans, small business owners, the CEOs of huge real estate companies. These people believed, as I do, that *how* they served their clients was as valuable as *what* they served. And they knew that what they could learn from leaders in my business could supercharge how they ran theirs.

When you create a hospitality-first culture, everything about your business improves—whether that means finding and retaining great talent, turning customers into raving fans, or increasing your profitability. It's my hope this book will be part of the movement ushering in this new era. But my motivation isn't your bottom line—or not my only one, anyway. Because what I'd really like to do is let you in on a little secret, one that the truly great professionals in my business know: **hospitality is a selfish pleasure**. It feels *great* to make other people feel good.

In this book, I'll share stories from the twenty-five years I've spent working every position in a restaurant, from dishwasher to owner, and everything in between. And I'll share the lessons I've learned about service and leadership through the lens of hospitality—the little ones, the big ones, and the little ones that turned out to be big ones. Everything, in other words, you need to turn the world from black and white to color for you, the people you work with, and the people you serve.

Welcome to the hospitality economy.

CHAPTER 2

MAKING MAGIC IN A WORLD THAT COULD USE MORE OF IT

FOR MY TWELFTH BIRTHDAY, my dad took me to the Four Seasons for dinner.

At the time, I had no idea the Four Seasons was the first truly American fine-dining restaurant. Or that the elegant, mid-century modern interior was so iconic, it would eventually be designated a landmark by the City of New York.

I didn't know that James Beard and Julia Child had consulted on the menu, or that President John F. Kennedy had celebrated his birthday there an hour before Marilyn Monroe serenaded him with "Happy Birthday, Mr. President." Or that celebrities, titans of industry, and heads of state could judge whether their star had fallen in the city's ever-shifting power rankings by how close their table was to the Carrara marble pool at the center of the room.

What I did know was that the Four Seasons was the fanciest and most beautiful place I'd ever been in my life.

I was glad I'd insisted my dad buy me a classic Brooks Brothers navy blazer with brass buttons for the occasion; this was a place you dressed up for. I remember watching, wide-eyed and openmouthed, as a uniformed server expertly carved my duck on a gleaming cart pushed right up next to our table. When I dropped my napkin on the floor, he replaced it with a *totally new one* and called me "sir."

"People will forget what you do; they'll forget what you said. But they'll never forget how you made them feel." This quote, often (but probably incorrectly) attributed to the great American writer Maya Angelou, may be the wisest statement about hospitality ever made. Because thirty years later, I still haven't forgotten how the Four Seasons made me feel.

The restaurant cast a spell I was all too happy to be enchanted by. It put the world on pause, so that everything else fell away; the only thing that existed for me, for those two and a half hours, was what was in that room.

That night, I learned a restaurant could create magic, and I was hooked. By the time we left, I knew exactly what I wanted to do with my life.

People Will Never Forget How You Made Them Feel

Both of my parents worked in hospitality.

They met in 1968, when my dad was working in Phoenix for Sky Chefs, American Airlines' catering arm. This was back when people dressed up to get on an airplane and the food they were served in the air was delicious.

My dad's distinctive Boston accent stuck out in Arizona, and one day, someone on his team said, "Hey, Frank: there's a woman on the plane who speaks the same language as you." He was talking about my mother, who also spoke with a thick Boston accent. She was a stewardess, which is what they used to call flight attendants in the bad old days, when they were weighed every week and weren't allowed to keep working after they got married.

The two Bostonians connected. My dad recognized my mom right away; as it turned out, the two of them had gone to grade school to-gether, where he'd nursed an enormous fourth-grade crush on her. She had no recollection of him whatsoever. He'd lost her when she'd disap-peared in middle school; her mother had passed away, and she'd moved to Westchester, just north of New York City, to live with relatives.

Suddenly, there she was again.

The two of them fell madly in love. (This was temporarily compli-cated by my dad's three years of army service in Vietnam, and the fact that both of them were engaged to other people when they met.) They were married in 1973.

My dad left American Airlines and moved around the restaurant busi-ness before taking a job as a regional vice president for Ground Round, an old-school, casual-dining chain known for passing out whole pea-nuts and encouraging patrons to throw the shells on the ground. They moved to Sleepy Hollow, New York. My mother kept her job, traveling all over the world (times had changed, and American had suspended the rules about married flight attendants). After I was born, my cousin Liz moved in to help take care of me while my parents were away for work.

My parents had a good life. They were happy at home, and they shared a ferocious work ethic, as well as an intense sense of pride in their careers. My mom finished college by putting herself through night school, and she even earned her pilot's license, though she was never a very good driver, which makes me wonder who thought it was a good idea for her to fly a plane.

Then, one day when she was working in first class, my mother dropped a cup of coffee.

Over the course of my career working in restaurants, I've dropped lots of things. But my mother maintained such a high standard of excel-lence that the incident stood out—even more so when, a few weeks later, she dropped another one.

That's when they went to see the first doctor.

A few months, and a hundred appointments and tests later, my mother was diagnosed with brain cancer. The disease had spread, so her doctors couldn't neatly remove the tumor; they'd need to use radiation to kill whatever parts of it they couldn't take out.

She had her first surgery when I was four years old. Afterward, she was in pretty good shape, except her face drooped on the left side, and she couldn't use her left arm or her left leg (which did not, incidentally, improve her driving). But radiation then was less precise than it is now, and when the radiation sickness kicked in, her condition began to decline.

She didn't let her steadily deteriorating health stop her from being a mom. She drove me to tennis practice a couple of times a week for as long as she could. When it got too difficult for her to get in and out of the front seat, she would drop me off and wait in the car for an hour and a half, patient while the New York winter raged around her.

She was like that. She loved me recklessly.

One night, she fell coming down the stairs. My dad was working restaurant hours, as he did for most of his professional life; when he got home around eleven, he found my mom and me sleeping on the bottom step. I was too little to help her up, but not too little to fetch us pillows and a blanket so we could make a comfy nest.

Eventually, my mom became a full quadriplegic. After that, she lost the ability to communicate. But she kept going; she kept *living*.

My dad wanted me to be as independent as possible given the circumstances, so he sold our house and moved us three blocks away from my school. That way, I wouldn't have to rely on other people to drive me around, and friends would naturally end up at my house. In junior high, I started playing drums. I played in punk bands, and ska bands, and funk bands—and we rehearsed in my room, which was right above the kitchen, where my mother hung out during the day. Listening to a crew of high school boys stumbling through the iconic opening chords of Nirvana's "Come as You Are" a thousand times would be a waking nightmare for most people. My mom loved it.

Eventually, home health aides came in to help with her care. Every single day, my mom would ask the aide on duty to push her wheelchair to the end of the road to wait for me. She could no longer speak or get up to give me a hug, but she could be there with a huge smile on her face when I got home from school. That smile was all I needed, and it taught me an invaluable lesson—what it's like to feel truly welcomed.

The Power of a Genuine Welcome

By the time I was a senior in college, my parents were living in Boston. My mom relied on a pretty complicated medical setup by then, so travel required specialized equipment and a medical van. I was playing in a sixteen-piece funk band called the Bill Guidara Quartet, and my mom hadn't seen me play music in years, so my dad had the idea he'd bring her to Ithaca to see me perform. The trip would also serve as a trial run for their upcoming trip to my graduation.

Smoking was still allowed in bars then, which wasn't going to work with my mom's medical equipment. So I talked the powers that be into letting us do a show at Willard Straight Hall, the student union community center at Cornell. It wasn't the show we usually did, but it was an incredible experience: I got to play Stevie Wonder's "Superstition" to my mom, sitting in her wheelchair in the crowd.

Her smile lit up the dark room.

The next term, my last one at Cornell, I took what turned out to be my favorite class: Guest Chefs, a spring-semester class run by a professor named Giuseppe Pezzotti, who was an absolute legend at the school.

As Cornell has evolved, it's become less about food and beverage programs at restaurants and hotels and more about real estate and consulting. But there was still a tiny group who were more interested in what it means to be a classic, old-school maître d' than in spreadsheets, and Giuseppe Pezzotti was our king. (To give you an idea: it was in his class I learned how to peel a grape with a fork and a knife.)

As far as I was concerned, Guest Chefs was the coolest class at Cornell because we got the experience of running a real restaurant. Every semester, a guest chef would come to do a dinner, staffed entirely by the students. One group of students would serve as the chef's management team, another group would work as kitchen staff, while the third group ran the dining room.

I was fortunate enough to be part of the management team for the great Daniel Boulud. Daniel is so renowned in my industry he is known by his first name alone; it is also the name of his Michelin-starred restaurant in New York, which he opened in 1993 after years as the acclaimed chef at Le Cirque. Since then, his empire has since expanded to *a lot* of restaurants, in places as far-flung as London, Palm Beach, Dubai, and Singapore.

He is unquestionably one of the most famous chefs in the world— and yet he was prepared to come to upstate New York to cook a meal as part of a college class. Later, I would learn this is entirely consistent with his character: Daniel is well-known for his generosity toward young people coming up in our industry.

I was assigned to be the marketing director for the dinner. There wasn't much marketing to do for a dinner with a chef as famous as Daniel; the dinner would sell out as soon as people heard he was coming. But I still wanted to do something cool. Knowing guests would want to watch him in action, I arranged for a chef's table in the kitchen—the first ever in the history of Guest Chefs. It was odd to see a formal table set up in the middle of the ugly, industrial hotel-school kitchen, so I put a red velvet rope around it to make it swanky.

We auctioned off the chef's table and raised a few thousand dollars for the charity Taste of the Nation. I was happy to attend their annual dinner a few weeks later to hand over a big cardboard check from Cornell, but I was most excited about playing host to the chef and his team. I didn't have much in the way of resources, but I was going to make sure they had a great time.

Daniel's advance team was scheduled to arrive on a Thursday. The two sous chefs were Johnny Iuzzini and Cornelius Gallagher. Johnny went on to a successful television career and to win multiple James Beard Awards as head of pastry for Jean-Georges Vongerichten's restaurants; Neil would earn three stars from *The New York Times* as the chef of Oceana, a temple to impeccable seafood in midtown Manhattan. At the time, though, the two of them were just kids, and I was a nerdy senior at hotel school trying to impress them. So when it was time to go pick them up from the airport, I borrowed an Audi A5 from the girl I sat next to. It was the nicest car in our class.

There aren't any fancy restaurants in Ithaca. If you want to show people a good time, you take them to the Pines—Glenwood Pines on Cayuga Lake. The Pines is known for its view and huge cheeseburgers served on French bread. Think jalapeño poppers, stained-glass Yuengling lamps hanging over the coin-operated pool table, a game on the TV behind the knotty pine bar.

The burgers did not disappoint, and the beers we had alongside didn't hurt, either. Afterward, my distinguished guests wondered if I happened to know where they could score some weed.

As a matter of fact, I did. The group ended up back at my house— 130 College Avenue, your quintessential college party house, complete with a janky pool table in the dining room and a pair of mildewing couches on the porch, where the party continued until the wee hours.

The next morning, I staggered off to class, while Neil and Johnny reported to the kitchen of the student-run Statler Hotel on campus to prep for the Guest Chefs' dinner. I didn't see them again until the evening, after Chef Boulud had arrived. I was incredibly nervous to meet him, but Daniel was charming right off the bat, and Johnny and Neil were obviously happy to see me again.

The dinner went brilliantly. Afterward, everyone—Daniel, Neil, Johnny, and most of our class—ended up, as was the custom, at Rulloff's, a dive bar near campus. As the night wore on and more (and more) friends showed up, it seemed natural to head back to my place, where we always had at least one keg stashed in the basement. But the crowd was getting snacky, and my kitchen cupboards—including the one whose door had been hanging from a single hinge since the day we moved in—were bare.

Which is how I found myself, three sheets to the wind at one in the morning, talking my way back into the kitchen of the Statler Hotel with Daniel Boulud.

"I am the chef from the event tonight," Daniel explained in his charming French accent as the two of us approached the front desk, "and I must get into the kitchen." Once in, we rounded up pans, butter, eggs, truffles, and caviar and headed back to 130 College Avenue.

So there was Daniel Boulud in my busted kitchen, drinking Milwaukee's Best from a red Solo cup and whipping up scrambled eggs with truffles for a bunch of wasted college kids. Did one of the most celebrated chefs in the world do a keg stand on my pool table? I'll never tell.

The party reluctantly broke up around three in the morning. We parted with hugs all around.

The Nobility in Service

A month and a half after the Guest Chefs' dinner, all the arrangements were in place for my parents to attend my graduation. Then, two days before they were set to leave, my mom slipped into a coma.

My cousin Liz drove out to Ithaca with her family in an RV so I wouldn't be alone for the ceremony. I threw my cap in the air, then ran straight to my car.

By the time I got to my mom's hospital room in Boston, it was late in the evening. My dad had gone back to the apartment already, and I fell asleep lying on my mom's bed. When I woke up in the middle of the night, she was awake.

What happened next was extraordinary. For the first time in six years, my mother was able to speak intelligibly. "You graduated?" she asked me, and I told her I had. We talked easily and for a long time. I didn't have to strain to understand her, and she didn't have to struggle to speak.

Eventually, she slipped away again. I ran to get a doctor: "She was awake!" But it didn't matter; she had fallen back into a coma.

The next morning, I went back to the apartment to see my dad. He was exhausted after logging serious hours by my mom's side at the hospital. In an effort to cheer both of us up, I suggested we hit the racquetball court for a quick game. Afterward, as we were getting changed, his phone rang. As soon as I saw his face, I knew my mom was gone.

I wrote a speech to give at her funeral, but when I got up to deliver it, the words I'd written didn't feel right. I ended up telling a couple of funny stories instead, including the fact that, despite the many challenges my mom had in communicating, she was always able to perfectly articulate my dad's credit card number whenever she shopped over the phone. Then we had a huge dance party. Instead of mourning her loss, we celebrated her life.

Much later, a guest at Eleven Madison Park would tell me that while most people save the best bottles of wine in their cellars for celebrations, he drinks his best bottles on his worst days. I thought of my mom's funeral immediately when he said that, because that was exactly what we did that night. The party was perfect; she would have loved it.

As anyone who has lost someone important knows, the days immediately after a huge loss can get very dark. Visiting relatives go home, the casseroles stop coming, and the immediate family is left alone. The shock wears off, and grief sets in.

The week after my mother died, I was supposed to fly to Spain for an internship, where I would be working as a prep cook in exchange for room and board at a hotel school owned by a former Cornell grad. But it didn't feel right to jet off to Spain a week after my mother's death. Mostly, I didn't want to leave my dad alone.

It was my dad who pushed me to keep the commitment. "What are you going to do, sit around here and be sad? Get on the plane. If you change your mind, you can always turn around and come home."

So in the middle of this intense mourning period, I started scrambling to make plans to travel to Spain. Even though I was in Boston, the only flight I could find last minute was out of New York's JFK, so my dad offered to drive me down.

That gave me an idea. With nothing to lose, I emailed Chef Boulud: "Is there any way I could bring my dad to the restaurant next Saturday?"

People wait months for reservations at Daniel, but the email I got back could not have been more gracious: "I would love to have you. You welcomed me into your home; now I will welcome you into mine."

My dad and I were running so late for the reservation, we had to change into our suits at a gas station off I-95. I didn't have the slightest idea what to expect, but even if we hadn't been going to one of the best restaurants in the world, I would still have been anxious: this was the first time in my life I was bringing my dad to a restaurant, as opposed to him bringing me to one.

At Daniel, the general manager greeted us at the door. "Chef Daniel is excited to have you with us tonight. Your table is right this way." He brought us through the bar, the formal dining room, into the kitchen, and upstairs into the Skybox, a luxurious, glass-enclosed private dining room that looks down over the kitchen, where forty cooks—and Chef Boulud—work in a state-of-the-art facility.

It's a once-in-a-lifetime table, and I was too stunned to speak. But the ice was broken immediately as Daniel's voice boomed over the intercom into the booth: "Willieeee!"

The kitchen proceeded to send us a series of exquisite courses, which Daniel personally spieled over the intercom as each plate arrived. As we tasted the delicious food, drank the superb wines, and experienced the warmth of Daniel's hospitality, I watched years of exhaustion and pain lift from my dad's face.

That night was the saddest I have ever been, or ever want to be, and the same was true for my dad. Yet, even in the midst of that sorrow, Chef Boulud and his staff were able to give the two of us what still feels like four of the best hours of my life. It's astonishing to me that one of the most famous chefs in the world stayed until the wee hours to give us a tour, but the meal was so beautiful and so long that by the time Daniel was embracing us goodbye, my dad and I were the last people in the entire restaurant—not the last guests, but the last people, period. There was no check.

I had already happily chosen a life in restaurants, but that night, I learned how important, how noble, working in service can be. During a terribly dark time, Daniel and his staff offered my dad and me a ray of light in the form of a meal neither one of us will ever forget. Our suffering didn't disappear by any means, but for a few hours, we were afforded real respite from it. That dinner provided an oasis of comfort and restoration, an island of delight and care in the sea of our grief.

When you work in hospitality—and **I believe that whatever you do for a living, you can *choose* to be in the hospitality business**—you have the privilege of joining people as they celebrate the most joyful moments in their lives and the chance to offer them a brief moment of consolation and relief in the midst of their most difficult ones.

Most important, we have an opportunity—a *responsibility*—to make magic in a world that desperately needs more of it.

CHAPTER 3

THE EXTRAORDINARY POWER OF INTENTION

GROWING UP, I WENT TO work with my dad every Saturday.

For most of my young life, my dad was the president of Restaurant Associates, a massive restaurant company that, over time, has been responsible for everything from corner coffee shops and corporate cafeterias to fine-dining establishments like the Rainbow Room—and the Four Seasons.

The restaurants my dad oversaw for RA—including Brasserie, the restaurants at Rockefeller Center, and the food and beverage program at Lincoln Center—were buzzy and busy. He'd often leave me for an hour with a cook or one of the servers, who'd give me a job to keep me busy. I loved the behind-the-scenes access and the surge of energy that coursed through me when I walked through those dining rooms.

When I was thirteen, about a year after our dinner at the Four Seasons (on the drive back from SeaWorld, of all places), my dad asked me what I wanted to do with my life.

This might seem like a crazy thing to ask a thirteen-year-old kid, but my dad was incredibly intentional with his parenting, as with everything in his life. Every day, he'd wake up, get my mom out of bed, put her in her wheelchair, help her in the shower, then make and feed her breakfast—all before heading off to work. Fifteen hours later, he'd come home and do it all backward, always finding the time to watch me perform a new song I'd learned on the drums or help me with my homework.

His stamina and selflessness were amazing to witness, but I now realize he never would have been able to achieve what he did as a businessperson, as a husband, or as a father without mapping out his days with precision, organizing his priorities, and setting his nonnegotiables. For my father, intentionality wasn't a luxury or business philosophy; it was a requirement.

I inherited from him an understanding of the importance of this concept—as you'll see, "intention" is a word I use a lot. **Intention means every decision, from the most obviously significant to the seemingly mundane, matters.** To do something with intentionality means to do it thoughtfully, with clear purpose and an eye on the desired result.

With that background, perhaps it's not odd I knew exactly what my life goals were, even at thirteen. First, I wanted to study restaurant management at Cornell University's School of Hotel Administration. Second, I wanted to open my own restaurant in New York City. Third, I wanted to marry Cindy Crawford.

Everything I did from that point forward was with those goals in mind, and I'm proud to say I achieved two out of three—and did better on the third. (No disrespect to Ms. Crawford, but my wife is *really* awesome.)

My real first job, at fourteen, was at the Baskin-Robbins in Tarrytown. I left many ruined cakes in my wake; it's harder to pipe "Happy Birthday" onto an ice cream cake than you think. In high school, I worked as a dishwasher and a host at the Westchester outpost of Ruth's Chris Steak House and, over a summer vacation, as a busser at Wolfgang Puck's Hollywood restaurant, Spago. Later, I would work as a server at Drew Nieporent's Tribeca Grill; I even spent a summer cooking at another Wolfgang Puck restaurant called ObaChine.

And in my senior year, I applied and got into the hotel school at Cornell University.

My dad pushed back on that decision. He wasn't entirely opposed to my choosing a life in restaurants, but he was uncertain about my committing to the path so early; a degree in hotel management would mean my career was laid out for me. (He also had some experience with Cornell graduates, who tended to come out of there believing they were ready for a CEO position, and he *really* didn't want me to be one of those assholes.) But when I was accepted, I knew I wanted to cross that goal off my list.

I loved Cornell and met some of my closest friends there. As graduation drew near, my friend Brian Canlis and I traveled down to Manhattan and worked our way uptown from Tribeca, stopping for a snack or a glass of wine at some of the best restaurants in the city: Nobu, Montrachet, Chanterelle, Zoë, Gotham Bar and Grill, Gramercy Tavern, Union Pacific, Tabla, and Eleven Madison Park. We kept going, up to Alain Ducasse, Café des Artistes, and more.

Of the many restaurants we saw, two—Tabla and Eleven Madison Park, both owned by the restaurateur Danny Meyer—stood out to me. It felt natural to be in their dining rooms, and I returned to school excited to learn more about them. As it happened, a couple of months later, Richard Coraine, one of his partners, came and spoke to one of my classes at Cornell, and I fell in love with their company, Union Square Hospitality Group.

At the time, Danny had only four restaurants—Union Square Cafe, Gramercy Tavern, Eleven Madison Park, and Tabla. Gramercy Tavern and Union Square Cafe were two of the most beloved restaurants in New York City, inevitably numbers one and two every year in the annual Zagat guide. Eleven Madison Park was a bustling brasserie in an extraordinary room—the vaulted, marble-clad former executive assembly room in a landmarked Art Deco building; Tabla, in a smaller, adjacent space, was the most exciting Indian restaurant in the country.

Danny had revolutionized fine dining in New York by putting a uniquely Midwestern spin on going out to dinner. His restaurants offered both a friendlier, more informal dining experience, and a more excellent one—largely because of the people who worked for him.

The cornerstone of the company's culture was a philosophy Danny called Enlightened Hospitality, which upended traditional hierarchies by prioritizing the people who worked there over everything else, including the guests and the investors. This didn't mean the customer suffered; in fact, the opposite. Danny's big idea was to hire great people, treat them well, and invest deeply into their personal and professional growth, and they would take great care of the customers—which is exactly what they did.

By the time I graduated from Cornell, there was no question in my mind: Danny Meyer was the guy to work for. And when I got back to New York from Spain, I landed an interview with Richard Coraine. Ironically, my interview took place at Eleven Madison Park, though Richard ended up offering me a manager position at Tabla. Before I accepted Richard's offer, though, I allowed myself one last moment of hesitation. Neither EMP nor Tabla was pretentious, but they were fancier places than I'd ever pictured myself working at; I was (and still am) more cheeseburger than foie gras.

Not for the first or last time, I turned to my dad for advice. He addressed my concerns this way: "It's easier to learn the right way to do things at the high end than it is to break bad habits. You can always take it down a notch later, but it's harder to go the other way."

A month later, I was a manager at Tabla, running the front-door team. My education had begun.

CHAPTER 4

LESSONS IN ENLIGHTENED HOSPITALITY

TABLA TRANSFORMED contemporary Indian cuisine in the United States—and the engine behind that transformation was Chef Floyd Cardoz, who cooked food inspired by his Goan heritage.

Eleven Madison Park and Tabla had opened at the same time, but EMP had gotten two stars from *The New York Times*, while Tabla had earned a coveted three. This was a huge win for upscale Indian cuisine, and a real tribute to Floyd's stubborn intensity and the true deliciousness of his food.

It was at Tabla that I learned the power of being the underdog. Despite its critical success, Tabla never did the business other restaurants in the company did, but Floyd insisted we wear our outsider status like a badge of honor. Meanwhile, he kept his head down, pumping out some of the best food in the city.

Floyd wanted the new dining room managers to respect what went on in his kitchen, so every one of us did a brief trail when we started. I showed up, naively assuming I was there to observe the cooks at work on the line; instead, I was ushered to the prep kitchen and given a bucket of shrimp to devein. I spent the next three hours elbow-deep in shrimp guts.

The next day, Floyd asked me to chop an onion. It was terrifying. I'd done a little cooking and attended some culinary classes in college, but I was pretty sure I wasn't going to do it to his standard, and I didn't. Floyd didn't yell, but he did toss my onion in the trash and take the knife out of my hand so he could show me how to do it correctly. Watching the intensity and respect and focus he brought to that most humble of kitchen tasks was a good preview for what was to come.

Tough as he was, it was impossible not to love Floyd and his huge grin. The childlike wonder on his face as he watched us taste a mind-blowing new dish for the first time was a gift as inspiring as his food.

Two things happen when the best leaders walk into a room. The people who work for them straighten up a little, making sure that everything's perfect—and they smile, too. That's how we were with Floyd. Tabla was his big crazy dream, and everyone who worked for him would do whatever we could to help him make it a success.

Go Above and Beyond

In *Setting the Table*, Danny Meyer's groundbreaking book about enlightened hospitality, he tells a story about a couple celebrating their anniversary at one of his restaurants. Midway through their meal, they remember they've left a bottle of champagne in the freezer. They call the sommelier over to ask if it's likely to explode before they get home (almost certainly yes). The sommelier saves the day by taking their keys and rescuing the bottle, so the couple can relax and finish their celebratory meal. When they arrive home, they find the champagne safely tucked into their fridge, along with a tin of caviar, a box of chocolates, and an anniversary card from the restaurant.

That story and many others like it circulated through the company. They primed every one of us to seek out new ways to make our guests' experiences a little more seamless, relaxing, and delightful. And so, the first time a guest mentioned she was going to have to get up, midmeal, to feed the meter a few blocks away, it was natural for us to offer to do that for her.

Eventually, that gesture became one of our steps of service. The host would ask guests, "How'd you get here tonight?" If they responded, "Oh, we drove," he'd follow up with, "Cool! Where'd you park?" If they told him they were by a meter on the street, he asked which car was theirs so one of us could run out and drop a couple of quarters into the box while they were dining.

This gesture was the definition of a grace note, a sweet but nonessential addition to your experience. It was an act of hospitality that didn't even take place within the walls of the restaurant! But this simple gift—worth fifty cents—blew people's minds.

Systemizing it turned it from an act of heroism into a matter of course, like checking your coat or offering a dessert menu. And the more normal it became for us to give this little gift, the more extraordinary it seemed to be for the people receiving it.

Enthusiasm Is Contagious

Randy Garutti, who went on to be the CEO of Shake Shack, was the general manager at Tabla when I started working there.

Randy was a wildly positive presence and an unabashed cheerleader for everyone who worked for him—the perfect foil for Floyd's intensity, and an ideal delivery system for Union Square Hospitality Group's signature combination of energy and integrity.

Danny's partner Richard Coraine would often tell us, "All it takes for something extraordinary to happen is one person with enthusiasm." Randy was that person.

He'd played competitive sports his whole life and brought both an athlete's tireless work ethic and a coach's sense of mentorship and team spirit to everything he did. His pre-meal meetings mimicked the rousing, before-the-big-game locker-room speeches you see in the movies and invariably ended with him pumping his fist at us in encouragement: "C'mon, guys, you've got this!"

Randy's animation was a wave that picked you up, whether you wanted it to or not, which was why he could face a crew of the distracted, the hungry, and the very-probably-hungover—and turn them into his own personal army. It was from him I learned: **Let your energy impact the people you're talking to, as opposed to the other way around.**

For a recent and slightly cynical college graduate, Randy's sunny optimism could sometimes stretch the limits of belief. Ask him how his day was going, and he'd say, "You know, man, I'm trying to make today *the very best day of my life.*" I might have rolled my eyes, but that kind of unwavering positivity turned out to be impossible to resist, largely because Randy believed every bit of what he was saying—and, before long, so did we.

Randy also instilled in us a sense of ownership by finding ways to demonstrate his faith in our judgment.

"You okay if I get out of here a little early?" he'd ask, tossing me the keys to the front door. As a twenty-two-year-old, I was thrilled to be left in charge. If the boss was gone, then *I* was the boss—which is why I worked harder when Randy was gone than when he was there.

More important, I never forgot how much his trust meant to me, which is why developing a sense of ownership in the people who worked for me would become a priority for me as soon as I was the one tossing the keys.

Language Creates Culture

Danny has always understood how language can build culture by making essential concepts easy to understand and to teach. He is brilliant at coining phrases around common experiences, potential pitfalls, and favorable outcomes.

These were repeated, over and over, in emails, in pre-meal meetings, and between staff members at USHG. "Constant, gentle pressure" was Danny's version of the Japanese phrase *kaizen*, the idea that everyone in the organization should always be improving, getting a little better all the time. "Athletic hospitality" meant always looking for a win, whether you were playing offense (making an already great experience even better) or defense (apologizing for and fixing an error). "Be the swan" reminded us that all the guest should see was a gracefully curved neck and meticulous white feathers sailing across the pond's surface—not the webbed feet, churning furiously below, driving the glide.

There were tons more of these, usually hooked to real-life stories, like the champagne rescued from the freezer. If you had one, you were encouraged to share it so it could become part of the canon, too.

Because of Danny's book *Setting the Table*, many of these concepts and catchphrases have made it into the culture at large.

My favorite was "Make the charitable assumption," a reminder to assume the best of people, even when (or perhaps *especially* when) they weren't behaving particularly well. So, instead of immediately expressing disappointment with an employee who has shown up late and launching into a lecture on how they've let down the team, ask first, "You're late; is everything okay?"

Danny encouraged us to extend the charitable assumption to our guests as well. When someone is being difficult, it's human nature to decide they no longer deserve your best service. But another approach is to think, "Maybe the person is being dismissive because their spouse asked for a divorce or because a loved one is ill. Maybe this person needs *more* love and *more* hospitality than anyone else in the room."

Restaurants are fast-paced work environments, so it was enormously helpful to have an established shorthand. The shared language meant we could offer better hospitality to our guests—and to one another. Because when you start focusing on extending the charitable assumption to the people around you, you find yourself giving it to yourself a bit more as well.

We were introduced to many of these concepts on our very first day, at the meeting for new hires. Those meetings were in themselves unusual; my Cornell friends had gone on to work for large restaurant companies who didn't do anything of the sort. And the importance of those meetings within USHG's culture sent an immediate signal: "There's a certain way we do things here, and it's bigger than teaching you how you move through the dining room or how to spiel a dish."

To begin, Danny would ask everyone to introduce themselves with a line or two. We got to know one another a little bit, which made it easy when we needed to ask for a favor or some advice (and came in handy when you were trying to impress a date and stopped by one of the other restaurants for a glass of wine).

But those introductions were also a meta-message. The fact that the head of the company was willing to use at least half of his meeting to take the time to hear from us individually made a big impression. It was our first indication that this central concept of enlightened hospitality— the idea that taking care of one another would take precedence over everything—was real.

For the rest of the meeting, Danny would walk us through every one of those phrases and the role they played in the culture, showing us right away that words mattered. He didn't focus on the what—he focused on the why. As a result, those meetings were more like class orientations at college than an introduction to company procedures.

Just being in the room felt like joining a movement or accepting a mission—a vibrant and exciting community more important than your-self.

"Cult" Is Short for "Culture"

Friends working at other large hospitality companies across the country could never believe my work stories. Some of them went so far as to make snide remarks: "Oh, you're working for the cult. . . ."

I knew what they meant; between the shared internal language, our avowed dedication to our bosses, and our unconventional commitment to taking care of one another, there was a slightly devotional feeling about USHG. But I have since come to realize that a "cult" is what people who work for companies that haven't invested enough in their cultures tend to call the companies that have.

Danny's management style made it cool to care, which probably did seem laughable if you worked for a different kind of company. But those of us who worked for him couldn't escape the positive repercussions of the culture he'd created, which was designed to make people feel good.

We were happy to come to work; our colleagues were happy to come to work. When our bosses walked in, we hustled a little harder—not because we were scared, but because we wanted them to see we were on top of our corner of the world. And every day, we saw guests leaving our restaurants contented, refreshed, and restored. They couldn't wait to come back, and neither could we.

This culture was strong, and it was working. Call it a cult! I was proud to be a part of it, and no amount of name-calling was going to convince me I was wrong.

So when Danny announced he was opening a restaurant and jazz club in the Flatiron called Blue Smoke and asked me to be the assistant general manager, I was thrilled. I'd been a musician all my life, and it was a great opportunity for a twenty-two-year-old.

Which begs the question: Why on earth did I say no?

CHAPTER 5

RESTAURANT-SMART VS. CORPORATE-SMART

"Before you fall head over heels with this one way of doing things, make sure you understand there are different approaches out there."

I was expecting my dad's excitement to match my own when I called him on my late-night walk home from dinner service at Tabla to tell him I'd been offered my dream job at Blue Smoke. Instead, in his calm, measured way, he questioned whether it was the best step for me to take—and listed all the reasons why it might not be. I listened, as I always did, because my dad didn't just give advice; he always took the time to explain *why*, a leadership skill I've always tried to emulate.

He knew how much I loved working for Danny Meyer and affirmed that what I was learning there, I couldn't learn anywhere else. But at the time, Danny's company had only four restaurants. Even if they were four of the best restaurants in the country, my dad was encouraging me to consider working for a bigger restaurant group—one with procedures and systems in place that USHG hadn't yet had the time to implement.

It was on that call that he introduced me to the concept of restaurant-smart vs. corporate-smart.

He described the distinction between the two. In the simplest terms: Where do the highest-paid people in the company work? In the restaurants themselves, or in the corporate offices? That says a lot about how the company is run.

In restaurant-smart companies, members of the team have more autonomy and creative latitude. Because they tend to feel a greater sense of ownership, they give more of themselves to the job. They can often offer better hospitality because they're nimble; there aren't a lot of rules and systems getting in the way of human connection. But those restaurants tend not to have a lot of corporate support or oversight—the systems that make great businesses.

Corporate-smart companies, on the other hand, have all the back-end systems and controls in areas like accounting, purchasing, and human resources that are needed to make them great businesses, and they're often more profitable as a result. But systems are, by definition, controls—and the more control you take away from the people on the ground, the less creative they can be, and guests can feel that.

Restaurant-smart companies *can* be great businesses, and corporate-smart companies *can* deliver great hospitality. But their priorities are different, in ways that fundamentally affect the guests' experience.

I could see my dad's point. Danny was the most restaurant-smart guy out there, but his company had grown organically, so there was very little big-company infrastructure in place. At the time, USHG didn't even have a corporate office; in fact, Danny's own office was just a room in the basement of Gramercy Tavern.

The people who worked for Danny had a tremendous amount of autonomy, which was fantastic for creativity—a chef didn't have to justify a special and expensive ingredient or fill out a thousand forms to clear it. But all that autonomy sometimes meant leaving money on the table, too. If all the chefs in the group were buying dishwashing detergent from different suppliers—which they were—the company had lost a valuable opportunity to collectively negotiate for a better price on an item that would have no impact on their guests.

My dad recognized that I was getting an incredible education in restaurant smarts with Danny's company. But he wanted me to one day run a company that was corporate-smart *and* restaurant-smart.

It was time to go get the other half of my education.

Control Doesn't Have to Stifle Creativity

Tabla was one of the hottest reservations in New York when I left my job there to go work for Restaurant Associates, my dad's old company, as the assistant purchaser and controller for the restaurants at the MetLife Building. In other words, I'd gone from the front door of one of the most glamorous restaurant jobs in New York to the basement at one of the least.

Ken Jaskot, the purchaser at RA, didn't need a full-time assistant, and the controller, Hani Ichkhan, didn't need one, either. So I split my days between them. From six a.m. to noon, I learned how to inventory a walk-in refrigerator, how to receive a delivery, how to calculate costs of goods sold, and how to order food and supplies. After lunch, I would take off my whites, put on a blazer and a tie, and start in with the numbers in the accounting department upstairs.

It's impossible to overestimate how important it was that I was doing both jobs simultaneously. Food and beverage costs average thirty cents out of every dollar a restaurant makes, and most of what lands in a walk-in won't last more than a few days. Oysters weren't theoretical to me as a luxury line item or a cell in a spreadsheet—they were the valuable, ugly little rocks I'd counted by hand earlier in the day, packed in ice, and nestled into their fish tub.

Upstairs, Hani made me run administrative reports pertaining to all aspects of the business—accounts payable, accounts receivable, payroll, food costs, and inventory—every single day. So I spent my mornings mak-

view, the Big Picture—a snapshot of the business that tells you what you're doing well, and what requires attention.

So the whole time I worked for Hani, I was desperate to get my hands on a P&L for one of the restaurants he oversaw. But he guarded those P&Ls like a dragon; I wasn't even allowed to look at them.

That didn't stop me from pestering him: "Can I see a P&L? Now?? Is it time?? What about now?" Every day, he told me to go run my reports.

Then one day, six long months in, Hani dropped a P&L in front of me. I'd hardly opened it before he started peppering me with questions, but he'd prepared me well; running those endless sub-reports meant I knew how to attack every problem that could possibly crop up.

And because I was working upstairs and downstairs, I had an almost preternatural sense for what the spreadsheets were telling me. Naturally our disposables line was high! But not because of waste or overordering; the company had sent us too many of our custom-printed to-go bags, and the guys downstairs had loaded them onto the shelves before we'd caught the mistake. So, yes, they needed to double-check the receipt before unpacking an order, but at least I knew why that line didn't look right.

I'm so thankful to have had a leader like Hani at that point in my life; there's so much I wouldn't have learned if I had skipped steps. I thought of him often, later in my career, when I was managing young people hungry for more responsibility or a bigger title. Hani hadn't been doing me a disservice by making me wait; he had been forcing me to strengthen my foundation, a solid base I relied on for years afterward. Waiting didn't dim my ambition or hamper my progress; it taught me to trust the process—a lesson I would see the wisdom of when I was showing my own staff that the right way to do things starts with how you polish a wineglass.

There's no replacement for learning a system from the ground up.

Sometimes Control Stifles Creativity

After nine months, RA moved me from my hybrid purchaser-controller assistant position and gave me another one: the assistant general manager and controller of Nick + Stef's Steakhouse at Madison Square Garden.

Nick + Stef's is an unusual restaurant, in that it's basically dead all the time—except right before a game at MSG, when it turns into one of the most popular restaurants in New York. Two hours before the game, people swarm in like locusts, order massive steaks and beautiful bottles of wine—then, ten minutes before tip-off, the whole restaurant stands up en masse and swarms out again. Because of that unevenness, everyone who worked there wore multiple hats—which made it perfect for me.

As assistant general manager, I ran around on the floor during the pre-game crunch, solving problems and helping servers. I was thrilled to be back in the dining room, talking to guests and fine-tuning their experience. During the off-hours, I did the restaurant's accounting, putting into practice everything I'd learned from Hani.

After two months, the changes I'd made had improved the restaurant's profitability by two points—and I was just as excited to run that report as I had been the first time I sent a host to top up someone's parking meter at Tabla.

Then, one afternoon, while helping out behind the bar, I realized that a floral display was blocking the bartenders' ability to make eye contact with the guests sitting at the two stools at the end of the bar. Easy fix: I moved the vase to the other side of the bar, where it looked just as good. As a bonus, the new placement blocked the guests' view of the busy and sometimes messy service bar, where servers stopped to pick up the drinks that bartenders had made for their tables.

Two days later, though, the arrangement was back in its original spot.

I asked my general manager why. "Arts and Design from corporate stopped by, and they weren't happy. You can't move stuff without asking them; that's not our job, it's theirs."

Wait, what? I couldn't move a *vase*?

At one level, I understood. When you have a lot of restaurants, you have to put some controls in place. I happen to have a decent sense of design, but not everybody does; you can't have random people making arbitrary decisions about how your restaurant is going to look.

Still. How could people in an office—who'd never been behind *any* bar, let alone ours—think they knew better than us about where that vase should be placed? The question nagged at me every time I saw that vase—and the bartenders craning their necks to see their guests around it. I had learned from Hani that corporate-smart didn't by definition stifle creativity. But that vase taught me that, left unchecked, it would.

Still, this was only a blip in an otherwise great experience, and I didn't dwell on it. I was still having fun on the floor on game nights and getting lots done in the back office.

Then, a month or two later, I ran into trouble with a server.

Let's call him Felix. Felix's type will be familiar to managers in every kind of customer-service business. They're notoriously disrespectful to their coworkers and often an absolute nightmare to work with, but they're considered unfireable because they're so beloved by the company's customers.

I have strong feelings about the Felixes of the world. **Just because a few regulars love an employee doesn't mean they should be allowed to erode the foundation of everything you're trying to build.** As charismatic and charming as these people may be with the public, and as valuable as the relationships they have with guests may seem, the collateral damage the Felixes do to the culture of a business is too dire to be tolerated.

One night, Felix rolled into work halfway through a dinner service, a full two hours late. That was a problem, because the dinner rush at Nick + Stef's before a game was no joke, even when we were fully staffed.

Still, when he walked through the doors, I channeled the charitable assumption. "Hey, I've been calling you. You had me worried—is everything okay?"

Without apologizing, Felix casually informed me that he'd "lost track of time." That was when I went from concerned to furious. "We've all been running our faces off, covering for you. Where have you been?"

"I don't need to explain that to you," he scoffed, pushing past me and heading toward the locker room.

"Don't bother changing," I called after him. "You're fired."

The next day, I got a call from Human Resources. "Felix called. We know he can be tough, but regulars love him and his check averages are routinely high, so we've made the decision to go ahead and rehire him. He'll be at work tomorrow; it would be great if you could apologize to him."

Again—at one level, I get it, I really do: a big company can't afford to have a twenty-three-year-old manager firing everyone who annoys him without cause. But whoever was sitting in that office reviewing how much food and wine Felix was selling on a spreadsheet could have no idea of the destructive impact he had on the team as a whole.

I did, and I was livid. Corporate-smart was all fine and good, but at what point do you need to trade some control in favor of trusting the people on the ground, the people who are connecting in real time with your team and your customers?

Former navy captain David Marquet says that in too many organizations, the people at the top have all the authority and none of the information, while the people on the front line have all the information and none of the authority. I was learning that, taken too far, corporate-smart could be restaurant-dumb.

I still stand by my decision to fire Felix. And I still feel that HR reversing my decision without consulting me—without even asking for my side of the story—was unacceptable.

I have thought of this experience many times when mediating disputes among my own employees. "We put our employees first" should mean *all* employees. Many misunderstood this about the first tenet of Danny Meyer's enlightened hospitality. When he said, "Take care of each other first," he didn't mean it was only a manager's job to take care of the hourly employees; it was everyone's job to take care of *everyone*.

Managers are employees, too. That doesn't mean they're automatically right or should be allowed to fire loyal, long-standing employees on a whim. But **if you take care of your managers and give them what they need to be successful, you put them in a better position to take care of their teams.**

After some grumbling, I brushed off the incident, figured out how to work with Felix, and got on with the job. But I'd be lying if I said that incident didn't change my relationship to my work. I felt disempowered, because I had been. And it was hard, from that disempowered position, to give all of myself—to spend twelve to fourteen hours a day executing someone else's vision—knowing that they'd had so little trust in me.

One afternoon a few months later, on a day off, I had lunch at Union Square Cafe, where my old boss Randy was general manager. (I didn't have a ton of money at the time, and eating where your friends work usually results in some free snacks.) Leaving the restaurant, I ran into Danny Meyer in Union Square. He didn't know me well, but we'd had a good relationship when I worked at Tabla, and we stopped to talk for a minute.

I wanted to stay connected to Danny because he was someone I admired. So a day or two later, I sent him an email, filling him in on what I'd been up to since I'd left Tabla the year before, including everything I was learning about accounting and purchasing.

Danny wrote back the next day, telling me in confidence that he'd signed an agreement to run the restaurants at the newly renovated Museum of Modern Art. "I'd love to talk to you about it sometime."

It was 2004, and MoMA was reopening after a two-year-long, $450-million renovation and expansion. Danny would be opening a high-profile fine-dining restaurant on the ground floor of the museum called the Modern, which would look out onto MoMA's legendary Sculpture Garden. The chef was Gabriel Kreuther, a rising star from Alsace who was one of *Food & Wine*'s Best New Chefs in 2003, and the dining room design was stunning—modern and serene. The Bar Room, a more casually designed area in front, would serve small plates and cocktails at the long, luxurious bar.

The Modern's opening would unquestionably be among the hottest and most eagerly anticipated of the year, but that wasn't what interested me. When I got Danny's email, my first thought was: *Whoa. They're taking over the restaurant operations of an entire museum. Imagine* that *P&L.*

And at our meeting, Danny proceeded to offer me the exact job I wanted: general manager for the casual food service operations in the museum. These included two cafés, where museumgoers could grab a salad for lunch or a cup of coffee as a pick-me-up; a staff cafeteria; and an in-house catering team that could service meetings and small gatherings. In other words, I would be responsible for everything except the fine-dining restaurant downstairs.

It was perfect. I had loved my time at Restaurant Associates, and I owe a lot of my success to what I learned there. I could easily have stayed with that company and gone on to do great things with them. But what Danny was offering me was truly unique and right up my alley: the chance to find out if I could bring corporate-smart to the most restaurant-smart company in the world.

Find the Balance Between Control and Creativity

I loved MoMA.

The museum staff had relocated to a satellite facility in Long Island City during the extensive renovation, so I was the first employee to have an office in the new museum. Coming into the empty building as the final pieces fitted together was the ultimate behind-the-scenes experience. The first couple of weeks, I passed Monet's *Water Lilies* every morning. It was leaning up against a wall, like the framed Pearl Jam poster I never got around to hanging in my college dorm.

My first office at MoMA was on the fifth floor. It was enormous—probably eight hundred square feet—and overlooked the Sculpture Garden. Before you get too excited, I was only up there because they were finishing the floors from the top down. When the museum staff started moving back into the building, I got systematically bumped down, floor by floor, like Milton in *Office Space*, until I ended up in the sub-basement. Which tells you how high-priority the food and beverage program was—at least, the food and beverage program I was responsible for.

That was true, even within my own company. Everyone at USHG was focused on what was happening down at the Modern and at the Bar Room, both of which were huge hits right out of the gate, equally and instantly adored by the critics and by the crowds.

The museum cafés, meanwhile, were the redheaded stepchildren of USHG, and I loved it. We were flying under the radar and had lots of creative freedom as a result. I immediately set out to implement my vision: to make the cafés at MoMA corporate-smart *and* restaurant-smart. But what I discovered almost immediately is that walking that line is really, really hard.

Every decision I made seemed to expose the natural tensions between

improving the quality of the experience the guests were having and doing what was best for the business. Restaurant-smart meant leading with
trust—including allowing the people who worked for me to do what they
felt was best for the guests. Corporate-smart meant running a tight ship.
Which was right?

One example, of many: our food costs in the cafeterias were high,
largely because of waste; we refilled the prepared-food cases with fresh
items right up until we closed, which meant we threw out a ton of food
at the end of the day. The obvious solution was to stop restocking the
cases at the end of the day, but I hated the thought of latecomers settling
for whatever sandwich or salad happened to be left over.

Hani would probably have sat down with the chef, Meg Grace, to
explain why she had to use ham instead of prosciutto. But that wasn't the
relationship I had with Meg, and it wasn't what either of us wanted for
our guests, either.

Meg and I found a compromise we could both live with: she'd keep
using expensive ingredients, and we'd stop topping up the cases an hour
or so before we closed—instead, we'd make all the salads and sandwiches
on the menu to order for people who came in during that final hour. The
labor costs were more than offset by what we saved on wasted food.

It was a step in the right direction, if not a perfect solution; I did
miss the orderly abundance of a fully replenished case. But the experience showed me that creativity was going to be the main ingredient in
striking a true balance between restaurant-smart and corporate-smart.

The Rule of 95/5

MoMa's Sculpture Garden is a unique New York space. Originally opened
in 1939, it was redesigned in 1953 by Philip Johnson (who also designed
the Four Seasons) as a "roofless room"—an ever-changing outdoor gallery

that would combine nature with architecture and art in a brand-new way. Massive sculptures rest on graceful, asymmetrical marble-paved areas, while birds sing from the plantings as if they don't know they're in the middle of Midtown.

There's nothing remotely like it in the city.

About a year into my job at MoMA, I was starting to get a little restless. I missed the energy of the opening; there's something magical about bringing a new idea to life, and I wanted that experience again.

So I became completely, utterly obsessed with designing a gelato cart for the Sculpture Garden. Since the cart would be sharing space with artwork by Henry Moore, Pablo Picasso, and Henri Matisse, not to mention rotating installations by contemporary artists like Richard Serra, everything about it would have to be perfect.

I needed the right partner, so I reached out to another notorious perfectionist: Jon Snyder, who owns il laboratorio del gelato, a company on the Lower East Side that makes small batches of dense, world-class gelato from chef-quality ingredients.

Jon jumped at the chance to be the official ice cream of MoMA's Sculpture Garden. Given the high-profile nature of the opportunity, I convinced him to pay for the cart and to give us a bargain-basement deal on his ordinarily very expensive gelato. (At that volume, he'd still do very well.)

We threw ourselves into the project. Jon proved to be an extremely dangerous co-conspirator. For example, he found a company in Italy making amazing, tiny blue spoons. How amazing could a plastic spoon possibly be? You're going to have to trust me on this: they were paddle-shaped, extraordinarily well designed, and completely unique. They were also preposterously, heartbreakingly expensive.

But I had to have them; the Sculpture Garden *deserved* them. Nothing else would do.

The first time my boss saw one of those spoons, she narrowed her eyes and asked me what they had cost. I told her, and her eyes got even narrower: "We'll talk about this later." But a month later, we sat down to review the first P&L for the cart, and I never heard another word about those spoons.

I'd managed 95 percent of my budget aggressively, leveraging MoMA's brand to get excellent gelato at a steep discount, and the beautiful cart for free. I'd earned the right to splurge on those spoons, the one small detail I believed would dramatically transform the experience of getting an ice cream at the cart.

This is what I would later call the Rule of 95/5: **Manage 95 percent of your business down to the penny; spend the last 5 percent "foolishly."** It sounds irresponsible; in fact, it's anything but. Because that last 5 percent has an outsize impact on the guest experience, it's some of the smartest money you'll ever spend.

This was affirmed for me one afternoon when I watched Glenn Lowry, the head of the museum, buy gelato for a group of visiting curators. Every single one of them spent a second or two admiring the spoons. I'd like to think some museumgoers went back to the cart for seconds, just because they loved that spoon.

The Rule of 95/5 would turn out to be one of my central operating principles at Eleven Madison Park. Wine pairings—a taste of wine to accompany each course in a tasting menu—are common in fine dining. And, as with everything, there was a budget for what we could spend on those pairings. But instead of splitting that budget evenly across all the wines we served, which is how it's often done, I'd ask our sommeliers to select slightly less expensive wines for the majority of the courses (these were no less excellent, because our wine director was so expert and our cellar was so diverse). Then, at the end, we could splurge on one special, rare, and more expensive glass.

If you love wine, it's always exciting to drink Grand Cru Burgundy. But the chance to do so almost never happens during ordinary wine pairings—so imagine how excited our guests were when it did! The Rule of 95/5 gave us the ability to surprise and delight everyone that ordered those pairings, making it an experience they would never forget.

The Rule of 95/5 extended to how we managed staffing expenses, too. My experience in Hani's office was never far from my mind when I was dealing with personnel; wherever we could, we worked to minimize expensive turnover and the dreaded overtime. But then, a few times a year, I would spend a truly obnoxious amount of money on an experience for the team, whether that meant closing the restaurant for a day so we could host a team-building retreat or hiring a DJ and buying a couple of cases of Dom Pérignon for the over-the-top staff parties we were famous for. The Rule of 95/5 ensured that I wasn't blowing the budget; I could afford these indulgences because I'd been so disciplined the rest of the year.

And when, at EMP, we threw ourselves into the concept of Unreasonable Hospitality, that 5 percent worked harder than it ever had before. One of my favorite examples: a family of four from Spain was dining with us on the last night of their New York City vacation. The children at the table were incandescent with excitement, and for the most wonderful reason: thick snow was falling past our massive windows, and they'd never seen real snow before.

Spur of the moment, I sent someone out to buy four brand-new sleds. After their meal was over, we had a chauffeur-driven SUV whisk the whole family up to Central Park for a special nightcap: a few hours of play in the freshly fallen snow. That 5 percent, spent "foolishly" (really, with tremendous intention), allowed us to create those special memories for our guests.

This rule played a huge role in my success, and its lineage can be traced directly back to the amazing education I received in the basements and back offices at Restaurant Associates. My dad, per usual, was right; I'm so glad he encouraged me to take that leap.

My experience at MoMA showed me that it *was* possible to be corporate-smart and restaurant-smart at the same time. The team was empowered, the guests were happy, and we were running a lean, mean, profitable business.

Then Danny asked to meet with me again.

CHAPTER 6

PURSUING A TRUE PARTNERSHIP

EVERYONE WHO WAS ANYONE IN Hollywood ate lunch at Spago, the crown jewel of an empire presided over by Chef Wolfgang Puck, who had revolutionized American dining by popularizing California cuisine.

I spent the summer there between high school and college, working as a busboy. Half a busboy, actually. Spago was a well-oiled machine, and the bussers were impossibly fast and clean and efficient. Since I could never hope to keep up with them, they gave me half a station; every other busser had fourteen tables, while I had seven. I did half the side work— the behind-the-scenes maintenance work required to keep a restaurant running smoothly, like polishing glassware and folding napkins—and received half the tips.

My dad had gotten me the job, so the team would have been well within their rights to roll their eyes while they were hazing me, but I was so excited to be there and worked so hard that everyone treated me like a kid brother.

Then, one afternoon during a busy lunch, I opened the door to the credenza in the dining room where the clean silverware, napkins, and plates were kept. The cabinet had been stocked so that a tall stack of bread and butter plates leaned precariously against the closed door; as soon as I opened it, those plates slid to the ground and shattered into a million pieces.

The crash was deafening, and the bustling restaurant fell silent for a second or two. A few people clapped.

The noise, the waste, the mess, the mistake—I was horrified. I certainly didn't need anyone else to be mad at me. Nevertheless, the kitchen doors flew open, and the chef de cuisine charged out of the kitchen, already screaming. At the top of his lungs and in front of everyone—my colleagues and all the guests—he told me exactly what he thought about my clumsiness.

The memory of the shame and rage I felt that day will always be on my shoulder when I'm handling a mistake made by someone on my own team. I never forget how much impact—for good or for bad—a gesture by a leader can have. And the big-picture message the chef de cuisine was sending was very clear: he didn't respect me or anyone else working in the dining room. In his view, fine dining was all about the food; we were just there in service of whatever magic he was making in the kitchen.

And I thought that sucked.

The duck I'd eaten at that dinner with my dad at the Four Seasons had been delicious, but it was part of a much bigger picture—the spectacular room, the artwork, the lighting, the floral arrangements, the table-cloths, the silverware, the staff's crisp uniforms—and the way the team had made twelve-year-old me feel like the most important person in the room. That combination had created an atmosphere of pure magic. The food was part of that magic, but it wasn't everything.

For most of the twentieth century, when you went out to dinner, you went to see and be seen; the chef's name wasn't on the menu. Beginning in the 1980s, though, with the advent of the celebrity chef, the pendulum had swung toward the kitchen. People were eating better food than ever before, but hospitality had taken a hit. I don't personally enjoy my steak

usually the chef. If I was going to go to Eleven Madison Park, I needed to know Daniel was willing to approach our partnership in a new way.

We met at Crispo, a lively Italian restaurant on Fourteenth Street, where we discovered a mutual love of pasta and Barolo. There were some similarities between us. I'd been working in restaurants since I was fourteen; so had he. We were both perfectionists, passionate about what we did, and unapologetically ambitious.

There were some major differences, too. Daniel had come up in Europe, working in extremely classic, Michelin three-star restaurants, while I'd been inventorying walk-in refrigerators at Restaurant Associates and learning a warmer, more relaxed form of hospitality under Danny Meyer. So we looked at the world—especially the world of hospitality—in very, very different ways. Ultimately, though, we felt our differences would be complementary.

We ended the night at a Dominican bar, two doors down from Crispo, drinking beers until late. It was there I told Daniel why I was so uncomfortable with the concept of fine dining.

"I love hospitality," I told him. "I want to make people happy. And I don't want to have to spend my whole life convincing you what I do is as important as what you do. If it's not a partnership—if what happens in the dining room doesn't matter as much as what happens in the kitchen—then I don't even want to start down this road."

More open communication between the kitchen and the dining room made sense to Daniel, too. He'd worked at one European restaurant where the culinary team *hadn't been allowed in the dining room at all*. Another installed a plexiglass window over the pass (the area in the kitchen where food is plated and finished before it's taken to the dining room), so the service team couldn't speak to the people working in the kitchen; instead, they communicated through notes.

That one hurt. The kitchen staff doesn't see the guests' faces light up with anticipation and appreciation when food arrives at the table, as servers and runners do; they don't see a diner swooning with pleasure at that first perfect bite. A chef shouldn't have to check the plates coming back to the dishwashing station to know whether a table liked their food.

By the time Daniel and I parted ways that night, slightly worse for wear, we'd made a decision that would guide our company's trajectory over the course of its lifetime: we'd decided we would be a restaurant run by both sides of the wall.

A restaurant driven by the chef was always going to do what was best for the food, while one driven by the restaurateur would always do what was best for the service. But if we had to make decisions together, we decided, we would end up with what was best for the restaurant as a whole.

CHAPTER 7

SETTING EXPECTATIONS

"To be the four-star restaurant for the next generation."

That was our first mission statement at Eleven Madison Park, and the one Daniel and I came up with most organically, over those first beers at the Dominican bar and any number of late nights after that.

At the time, the fine-dining scene in New York was in flux. Many of the old-school, classic white-tablecloth establishments in New York, like Lutèce and La Caravelle, had closed; people, especially younger people, didn't want that kind of stuffy formality anymore.

Some high-end restaurants were thriving, but even the ones we loved, like Jean-Georges and Daniel and Per Se and Le Bernardin, were owned and run by people twenty-odd years older than we were. While they had legions of devoted regulars, those restaurants were stalwarts, not the vanguard. Beloved as they were, they weren't at the center of the conversation.

Meanwhile, Daniel and I were in our twenties, and people our age were most excited about places characterized by irreverence and informality. Babbo's pasta was impeccable—and you ate it listening to *Led Zeppelin IV* turned up loud. At Ssäm Bar, the first thing you saw when you walked in the door was a life-size photograph of the combative tennis player John McEnroe—and that photo was the only decoration in the room. Prune's dining area was the size of a New York apartment bed-room, the open kitchen so close a line cook could and did reach over the pass to place a bowl of olives on your table. And the most precisely made and innovative cocktails in the world could be found at a speakeasy you entered through a phone booth in a hot dog joint in the East Village.

These restaurants paved the way for what was to come a few short years later: Kung Pao Pastrami at Mission Chinese and the Cheezus Christ pie at Roberta's, a barely converted, concrete-floored, graffiti-covered former warehouse in Bushwick. These restaurants served the best food the United States had to offer and fundamentally changed American dining. Owners spent money on ingredients, not fancy glass-ware, and the servers they hired were more likely to be pierced and tat-tooed than French and tuxedoed.

But, as wonderful as the food at those spots could be, a huge part of the hospitality experience was missing. The bo ssäm at Momofuku was a pork shoulder, cooked for hours, which you wrapped in lettuce at the table with oysters. It was, hands down, one of the most delicious dishes you could eat in New York. But the restaurant didn't take reservations, and there was no room inside the crowded restaurant to wait. So if you wanted that slow-roasted pork, you had to stamp your feet for an hour outside in the February cold—and when you were seated, it was on a knocked-together plywood stool without a cushion or a back.

Daniel and I had a vision for a fine-dining restaurant where we could have a good time without feeling like some grown-up was going to rap our knuckles for not sitting up straight. But we wanted to do it without sacrificing any of the exceptional amenities and glorious traditions of ser-vice that make a fine-dining meal so memorable and special. We wanted to marry the care and attention, not to mention the excellence and lux-ury, of classic four-star dining with the surprise and delight—the *fun*—of a more casual experience.

We wanted to make fine dining cool.

That was the dream, anyway. In reality, we had a ways to go.

Reconnaissance Matters

You should never waste an opportunity to gather intel before your first day on the job.

Luckily, I had an ace advance team already in place at EMP. Sam Lipp, an enthusiastic guy with an unrivaled passion for making people happy, had gone over to EMP a few months before, along with our colleague Laura Wagstaff; the two of them had been among my best managers at MoMA. So before I started, I took Laura out for a drink.

Laura is relentlessly can-do, a brilliant problem-solver, and a tireless advocate for the people who work for her, which is why I'm never happier than when she's next to me, whispering in my ear. It's Laura who tells me when a staff member needs a little TLC, when I'm being too intense, and when my attention is on the wrong thing. She's the one who taps my shoulder and says, "Hey, this needs a little finessing," or "You gotta chill out a little bit." (If it isn't already clear, I think every leader should have a Laura—someone who feels comfortable telling you when you aren't acting as the best version of yourself.)

The other thing about Laura? She never complains. Ever. So when she was shaking her head over her cocktail, telling me that what was going on at EMP was bad, I knew it was bad.

Or, in her words: "*bad* bad."

The first problem, she said, was that two factions had developed among the people who worked there.

The first faction was the old guard, servers and managers who had been working at the restaurant for years. EMP only had two stars in those early years, but it was a popular, busy restaurant with a ton of devoted regulars, which meant a server could make a healthy living working there. And the style of service had matched the food, which is to say that it was friendly and relaxed, without a lot of focus on precision or finesse.

The other faction was the fine-dining squad, the managers who had come in with Daniel. They came from prestigious restaurants all over the country, and they knew EMP could be exceptional. Unfortunately, they weren't doing a very good job of bringing the existing staff along to their style of service, or of helping the folks who weren't suited to that kind of service to find another place to work. They wanted the staff to be doing things their way—the "right" way—and were constantly irritated every-one wasn't living up to their exacting standards.

So the servers and managers who had been running the restaurant for years and were proud of everything they'd created felt unsettled and dis-respected, while the fine-dining squad was frustrated by the lack of prog-ress toward excellence.

In short, everyone was pissed off.

The friction within the team was aggravated by the fact that the res-taurant was badly disorganized. There were plenty of standards in place, but no real systems to communicate them. Unsurprisingly, this led to *a lot* of inconsistency.

My first week there, I watched a dining room manager correct the way a server was carrying a tray. The poor guy hadn't made it another ten steps before another manager stopped him and told him to hold the tray the way he'd been holding it in the first place. A minor inconsistency, fine—but if the managers couldn't agree on how they wanted a tray car-ried and communicate it to the people carrying them, what hope could there possibly be for the larger vision?

Meanwhile, a menu that had been more or less static for years was now changing all the time. Many of the purveyors were special and new, and the type of guest who was excited about Daniel's food *did* want to know which upstate farm the chèvre came from, and which hillside herbs the little goats were snacking on in the spring. But information—and there was a ton of it, including a huge and rapidly evolving wine list—came in on the fly, in an intense barrage nobody could be expected to absorb, especially twenty minutes before they were expected to share the excitement with guests.

Plus, the room had the same number of seats as it had when EMP had been slinging steak frites. It's not unusual, at even the best-run restaurant, for there to be a moment of real hustle on Saturday night at prime time; it's part of what makes restaurant work so fun. But there's also a reason you don't see four-star restaurants with a hundred and forty seats; you simply cannot serve that type of food—or deliver that level of service—at brasserie volume.

So basic service, the black-and-white piece, had slipped. Guests were waiting past their reservation times and too long for food when they were finally seated. During the worst nights, the whole bar would be packed with people running out of patience.

One weekend, there was such a disparity between the number of reservations the restaurant was taking and what the kitchen was able to put out, the team began humming the Guns N' Roses song "Welcome to the Jungle" when they ran into one another at the service station. They were supposed to be delivering an elegant, gracious experience, but a dining room manager turned to Laura and said flatly, "We might as well be working at Denny's."

Because it was a Danny Meyer restaurant, the team was quick to respond with complimentary champagne, along with lavish apologies for the wait. But there are only so many glasses of bubbles you can pour, or drink. People were coming to dine at the new EMP either because they loved Danny Meyer's restaurants or because they'd heard great things about Daniel's food. In either case, they were leaving disappointed. The restaurant was making more people mad than happy.

Invite Your Team Along

There's a fascinating and possibly overlooked advantage that businesses with strong cultures have: when an employee comes up in the organization, any other way of doing things just feels wrong.

And *wrong* is how EMP felt when I walked in on my first day.

In retrospect, I can now name everything that was going sideways and tell you what I did by way of correction. In the heroic version of this story, I struck a masterful pose and enumerated a number of inspirational management tenets, all of which transformed the restaurant within the week.

But the truth is, Danny's way of doing things—the way he treated his employees and guests—was so baked into my consciousness that for the first few months I was acting on instinct alone.

Mostly, the team needed to be brought along. They needed to feel seen and appreciated. They needed expectations to be clearly laid out and explained. They needed discipline to be consistent. They needed to feel like vital and important parts of an exciting sea change, not obstacles to making it happen.

From a management perspective, we needed to return to first principles, and at Union Square Hospitality Group, the first principle is *to take care of one another.* The fine-dining squad hadn't come from within USHG—and even if they had been able to absorb this crucial, employee-centered aspect of the culture, they'd been so focused on making their mark on the restaurant that they'd let this central principle fall by the wayside. That's why Danny had insisted the next GM come from within the company; for him, that aspect of the culture was not negotiable.

To bridge the gap between the two factions, improving communication was going to be key. At the same time, we needed systems, so everybody would know what they were supposed to be doing and how they were supposed to be doing it.

It was my hope that both fixes would make the team feel safer—and inspire them to come along on our mission. There was a lot to be done to make the restaurant better, but there would be no point to doing any of it if the people who worked there didn't love coming to work. If I couldn't succeed in getting hearts and minds on board for the bigger project, then the grand vision of a push toward excellence would be dead on arrival.

Leaders Listen

I had heard through the grapevine that, a few years before, a guy called Christopher Russell had made a big impression on his team with his first speech as GM at Union Square Cafe. (I wasn't there, so I'm paraphrasing.)

He said: "I am so excited to be here; I believe in and love this restaurant with all my heart. I'm also clear about what my job is, which is to do what's best for the restaurant, not to do what's best for any of you. More often than not, what's best for the restaurant will include doing what's best for you. But the only way I can take care of all of you as individuals is by always putting the restaurant first."

I *loved* this. It was a profoundly confident display of leadership—both a rallying cry and a way of telling the team, right away, exactly what they could expect from him as a leader.

I was inspired to use that same approach as a template for my own first-day speech. Except that Christopher had worked as a server and a manager at Union Square Cafe for years before that promotion. He knew every inch of the restaurant, and every one of the people in that room, down to their favorite cocktails and the names of their pets. People trusted him. He'd earned the right to give that speech. I hadn't.

Some of the best advice I ever got about starting in a new organization is: **Don't cannonball. Ease into the pool.** I've passed this advice on to those joining my own: no matter how talented you are, or how much you have to add, give yourself time to understand the organization before you try to impact it.

Having eyes and ears on the ground, especially those I trusted as much as Laura and Sam, was a gift. But aside from the insights they'd given me, I didn't know *anything*. So while I was tempted to deliver a similar rousing first-day speech about where the restaurant was going, I first needed to know where it was at.

One of the hardest parts about being dropped into a new environment is everyone is telling a different story. You have to connect with everybody and accept it might take a minute to determine if that manager really is a horrible person or if his agenda just differs from whoever's doing the complaining. **You're not always going to agree with everything you hear, but you've got to start by listening.**

In those early months at EMP, there was lots of finger-pointing and plenty of blame to go around; I've never been in a situation where it was so clear everyone was wrong *and* right at the very same time. Some of the old guard *were* phoning it in—and yet, it wasn't hard to see why so many of them thought the fine-dining crew needed to chill out.

It didn't even matter who was right and wrong, though, because *nobody* was communicating effectively. The front-line staff weren't talking to one another because nobody was talking to them, and they weren't listening to one another because they felt like nobody was listening to them. So I spent my first few weeks sitting down with every single member of the team and hearing them out.

That was a whole education in itself; I learned a lot of information about the restaurant it would otherwise have taken me a long time to figure out. Those meetings also taught me that time spent goes a long way. Sitting down with people shows them you care about what they think and how they feel and makes it that much easier for them to trust that you have their best interests in mind.

For this reason, I'd later ask the managers to stop sitting together during family meal, which the staff shares together before the restaurant is open. By spreading out, they'd learn, as I had, that the meal is a perfect opportunity to gather ideas and perspectives that might otherwise slip through the cracks.

Find the Hidden Treasures

My dad had his own platoon in Vietnam. He'd be the first one to tell you it wasn't a great one—in fact, it's highly likely he got it because nobody else wanted it.

In the platoon, there was a guy they nicknamed Kentucky, after his home state. Kentucky was lazy and wasn't in great shape; he had no hand-eye coordination, and terrible aim. And he was not the brightest bulb on the string; in the early days, my dad says, he wasn't sure Kentucky was plugged in at all.

My dad channeled his initial frustration into getting to know the team. Talking to Kentucky, he learned the kid had lived his entire life in the dense, deep backwoods of the rural South and that his supernaturally good sense of direction had been honed by a lifetime of navigating that land. Which also meant that, no matter how dark it got in the jungles of Vietnam, no matter how thick the foliage or how confusing the terrain, Kentucky could always find his way—in stark contrast to my dad and all the other city slickers, who were encountering those conditions for the first time.

So my dad moved Kentucky from the middle of the pack, where he'd been put as damage control, up to the point—the very front—where he excelled for his whole tour. In getting to know the guy, my dad turned one of the worst guys in the platoon into one of its strongest assets.

In business, he'd tell me, you choose your team; even if you inherit them, you decide if you want to keep working with them or not. In war, your team is assigned to you, and you can't fire anyone, and many of them don't want to be there at all. And the consequences of a poor decision in Vietnam were considerably more severe than a plate of food ending up in front of the wrong guest.

A leader's responsibility is to identify the strengths of the people on their team, no matter how buried those strengths might be.

I thought about that often when I was sitting down with the new team at EMP. It was tempting to weed out everyone who had a reputation as a less-than-stellar employee; eventually, some folks *would* need to be managed out. But first, I needed to make sure a hidden capability wasn't lurking behind someone's subpar performance.

Eliazar Cervantes was having issues in his role as a food runner; his managers repeatedly complained he didn't care. Which was true in a way, because Eliazar wasn't particularly interested in learning about the food. Of course he couldn't remember how old the balsamic vinegar was; he wasn't passionate about it.

After spending time with him, I discovered something about him others hadn't. He was incredibly organized and a natural leader, the kind of person who carried authority easily, and who could keep a steady hand on the wheel, even when it felt like the whole enterprise was headed off the rails. The solution wasn't to reprimand or fire him, but to give him a different role.

Eliazar became an expeditor in the kitchen. The expeditor is the person who tells the cooks when to start preparing the food and makes sure each dish gets to the right person at the right table in a timely fashion. A good one will know exactly what a table ordered, where they are in their previous course, and how long their entrées will take to cook. At a restaurant like EMP, he might be holding thirty different tables in his head at any moment.

In other words, the expeditor both conducts a symphony every night—and makes sure the planes don't collide in midair. It is one of the most important jobs in any restaurant, and one of the hardest.

And watching Eliazar do it was like seeing someone play chess in three dimensions. Once he'd moved from a position with no organizational component or opportunity for leadership into one that depended on those skills, Eliazar quickly came into his own, and the whole restaurant got to see his genius.

He went on to shine as head expediter at Eleven Madison Park for years, becoming an essential part of our success. Finding his hidden gifts, and those of others on the team, was an important step. The pieces were starting to come together.

Keep Emotions Out of Criticism

You know when one of your friends has fallen out of love but can't quite get it together to have the tough conversation with their partner about why the relationship isn't working? So they act like a giant jerk instead, in the hopes that the other person will get fed up and do the dumping? There had been a lot of that going on, managerially speaking, under the previous regime at EMP.

So I let the team know I wasn't afraid to have difficult conversations— hearing difficult things, or saying them.

The most valuable class I took at Cornell was Spanish, and the second most valuable was the one where I learned Excel. But I also have to give some credit to a class called Organizational Behavior—mostly because they made us read *The One Minute Manager* by Ken Blanchard and Spencer Johnson.

I still give *The One Minute Manager* to every person I promote. It's an amazing resource, in particular on how to give feedback. My biggest takeaways were: **Criticize the behavior, not the person. Praise in public; criticize in private. Praise with emotion, criticize without emotion.**

When someone who worked for me did a task well, I made sure to find a way to hype them up for it, and in front of as many of their colleagues as I could. Receiving praise, especially in front of your peers, is addictive. You always want more.

To ensure we were doing it consistently, we instituted the monthly Made Nice Award, where the entire management team voted for one person from the kitchen and one person from the dining room who had gone above and beyond—whether with a guest or for their colleagues.

This was inspired by the Employee of the Month awards you see at places like McDonald's. Those awards are usually unloved—four months out of date and hanging in a cheesy frame outside the bathroom—but it's amazing to **establish a regular rhythm for giving praise**.

We posted the Made Nice Award with the employee's picture above the time clock, so they'd enjoy the recognition of their peers. We also gave them a hundred-dollar gift card to the restaurant—a way for them to show off where they worked to their friends and family.

We were as thoughtful about criticism as we were about praise. I invited people on the team to come to me if they thought we could be doing something better, and to do so well before their frustrations reached a boiling point. Similarly, I encouraged managers to address their own issues with the team as soon as one popped up—before the problem became entrenched, and therefore emotionally charged.

When young managers take the reins of power—and most managers in our business are young when they start because of how little money they make—they want to be liked. They work with people fourteen hours a day, and often they end up going out for a drink after work; it's normal to want to be seen as part of the group.

So when a server comes in with an unironed shirt, you let the minor infraction slide in the interest of creating a friendly environment, both for the server in question and—let's face it—for yourself. You don't say anything. And you don't say anything when you notice the shirt isn't ironed the next day, and the next day, and the next.

By day twenty, you've started to take those wrinkles personally. The reality is that this guy hasn't ironed his shirt because nobody's told him to. But in your mind, he's not ironing his shirt because he doesn't respect you as a manager, or the restaurant he works at, or the other members of his team. That sloppy shirt has become a blinking neon sign for you: this guy couldn't care less about the amazing organization you're trying to build.

Your resentment festers, so by the time you eventually get around to addressing this unironed shirt issue with your employee, it feels personal—and emotional. Spoiler alert: the conversation you finally end up having with him is going to go badly.

At our manager meetings, we talked about how to avoid moments like this. Many of these confrontations could be avoided with early, clear, and drama-free corrections—like pulling that guy with the wrinkled shirt aside on day one to say: "Hey! Good to see you this morning. That shirt's looking a little rough; why don't you head upstairs and give it a once-over with the iron before we sit down for family meal?"

Every manager lives with the fantasy that their team can read their mind. But in reality, you have to make your expectations clear. And your team can't be excellent if you're not holding them accountable to the standards you've set. You normalize these corrections by making them swiftly, whenever they're needed.

And make those corrections *in private*. I can still feel the flush of shame and horror that crept up from my collar when I was screamed at in the dining room by the chef de cuisine at Spago; I'll remember it for the rest of my life. And while it was a terrible experience, it was also a privileged peek at a mistake I never wanted to make.

Correct an employee in front of their colleagues, and they'll never forgive you. In fact, the wall of shame that goes up may mean they can't even absorb what you're telling them. Issue the same correction in private, though, and it's a different exchange.

Whether criticism or praise, it's a leader's job to give their team feedback *all the time*. But every person on the team should be hearing more about what they did well than what they could do better, or they're going to feel deflated and unmotivated. And if you can't find more compliments to deliver than criticism, that's a failure in leadership—either you're not coaching the person sufficiently, or you've tried and it's not working, which means they should no longer be on the team.

These rules help your team to feel safe—especially if you practice them consistently. Consistency is one of the most important and underrated aspects of being a leader. A person can't feel safe at work if they're apprehensive about what version of their manager they're going to encounter on any given day. So if you're the boss, you need to be steady, controlling your moods so you don't end up taking out that morning's squabble with your spouse on a server with a wrinkled shirt.

This is the ideal but let's be honest: every once in a while, **you're going to mess up. When you do, apologize.** There's an inherent intensity that comes with being passionate about what you do, and on occasion, it can get the better of you. I've certainly expressed exasperation and disappointment in ways that weren't textbook illustrations of how to handle a correction in the workplace. But every time, I've made sure to apologize—not for the feedback itself, but for the way I delivered it.

Thirty Minutes a Day Can Transform a Culture

In spite of this mushy talk about listening and learning, at heart, I'm a systems guy. And in 2006, EMP desperately needed some systems.

When initiating change, I look for the best lever, whatever will allow me to transmit the most force with the least amount of energy.

And there's no better lever than a daily thirty-minute meeting with your team.

Most restaurants hold a daily meeting before service. It's called line-up or pre-meal and is a time to introduce and review new menu items, new wines by the glass, and new steps of service.

But it can be much, much more than that: **A daily thirty-minute meeting is where a collection of individuals becomes a team.** In fact, I firmly believe that if every dentist's office, every insurance company, every moving company had a daily thirty-minute meeting with their team, customer service as we know it would profoundly change.

At EMP, the way we ran our pre-meal meetings set a tone that was at least as important as what we said. Attendance was mandatory. The meetings started on time, at eleven and five, and lasted exactly thirty minutes. For the first year, I ran every single meeting myself, both lunch and dinner, Monday through Friday. I wanted the team to see me, and to know I was accessible and accountable to them, and consistent—that I'd do exactly what I'd said I would do, when I'd said I would do it.

In the restaurant's previous iteration, pre-meal had been exclusively devoted to the items on the plate or in the glass: here is the main ingredient, here's how long it was aged for, here's what it's served with, and this is how you pour the sauce tableside.

This basic transfer of information was vitally important, especially because so much was changing. At Danny Meyer's other restaurants, managers offered printed line-up notes, including new menu items, new wines, and information about new farms and producers, so the material could be taken and studied at home. But, probably because they were moving so fast, that practice had fallen by the wayside at EMP.

I immediately reinstituted it: there would be no more ambiguity about what we expected the servers to know. All the menu and wine descriptions had to be carefully written out, edited, and spell-checked by the managers, who were expected to have their packets ready on time for the meeting so servers could take notes in the packet during the verbal presentations made by the kitchen team and the wine director.

I stayed late every night that first week designing a template for those line-up notes, so they would be beautiful as well as clear and well-organized. That was unreasonable, but **the way you do one thing is the way you do everything**, and I wanted those notes to be as thoughtful, as beautifully presented, as the lavender honey–glazed dry-aged duck we brought to our guests. In this case, the people on staff were the recipients of my hospitality, and I wasn't going to stand up and talk about excellence without modeling it myself.

Done right, a pre-meal meeting fills the gas tank of the people who work for you right before you ask them to go out and fill the tanks of the people they're serving.

Communicating consistent standards, with lots of repetition, was important; a good manager makes sure everyone knows what they have to do, then makes sure they've done it—that's the black-and-white part of being a leader. But a huge part of leadership is taking the time to tell your team *why* they're doing what they're doing, and I used pre-meal to get into that why.

I spoke to the spirit of the restaurant and to the culture we were trying to build. I used those meetings to inspire and uplift the team and to remind them what we were striving for. Those thirty minutes were our time to celebrate the wins, even the small ones, a time to publicly acknowledge when someone on the team was crushing it.

Our meetings followed the same template every day, so everyone knew exactly what to expect. We'd start with housekeeping ("Thursday's the last day to make changes to your health insurance; call Angie if you've got questions"). Then I'd move into a quick riff on a topic that had inspired me. It could be an article I'd read about another company or a service experience I'd had somewhere else.

Inspiration was everywhere. One day, the place where I ordinarily got my hair cut was fully booked, so I stopped into a classic New York City barbershop, complete with twisting striped pole and combs soaking in huge blue jars of Barbicide. As I was paying for my haircut, the gruff barber asked me, "What do you want?"

I looked up, confused; he was pointing at three huge handles filled with gin, vodka, and whiskey. "Whiskey!" I said, grinning, and he handed me a shot in a tiny disposable cup, the kind your dentist uses for mouthwash, before sending me on my way.

I told the story that afternoon at pre-meal. Who on earth thought of that mini-shot? It was ridiculous, irrelevant, whimsical. A tiny dose of generosity designed to—what? To surpass your expectations, to change your channel, maybe just to put a smile on your face as you were walking out the door. It was wonderful, and I wanted the team to be as inspired by it as I had been.

The beginning of every pre-meal started with a call-and-response: "Happy Wednesday!" "Happy Wednesday!" They ended with one, too; I'd say, "Have a good service!" to which the staff would respond, in the tradition of the French kitchen, "Oui!"

You knew when you'd given a good pre-meal by the way they said "Oui!," and I got a good one that day.

Stealing thirty precious minutes for pre-meal from an already overcrammed day was a big ask, and sometimes my insistence on these meetings felt like rearranging the deck chairs on the *Titanic*. This was especially true because the managers immediately let me know that taking the full thirty minutes for the meeting would mean less time for side work, which was already squeezed into a slot too tight for everything to get done.

The answer, for me, was easy. "So let's dial back on some of this side work to make the time."

In order to become a team, we needed to stop, take a deep breath, and communicate with one another. If that meant using a more basic napkin fold or simplifying the butter presentation so everyone had time to meet, then that was a trade-off I was willing to accept. How connected we were as a team was more important to me than anything.

Set Them Up to Succeed

In those early days, I sat down with one server, a smart, personable guy who should have been perfectly suited to our new mission. At our meeting, though, he seemed drained and overwhelmed.

When I asked what was up, he pushed a giant packet of paper across the table—the notes he'd been given on the wine list. "I just don't think I'm going to be able to get on top of this," he said, and I couldn't blame him; I was lost myself by page three.

Employees who aren't succeeding tend to fall into two camps: the ones who aren't trying, and the ones who are. The end result may be similar, but the two need to be handled differently: you've got to move heaven and earth to help the people who are trying.

This was one of those times. Yes, I wanted EMP to have one of the best wine lists in the world and knowledgeable servers who could expertly guide our guests through it, but drowning them in detail wasn't the way to get there. Expectations were too high. We needed to solidify our foundation before adding more stories. We needed to slow down to speed up.

Later, this would become one of our catchphrases. I would remind the team: "You're busy, and there are a thousand things you need to do for your tables. But take ten seconds to double-check the order you've put into the computer, because entering the wrong dish has the potential to ruin your whole night—and that of your guests! Go too fast, and you'll end up slowing the whole restaurant down."

There was no way I was going to stop all forward progress toward a more refined, high-end service experience; there were a bunch of us,

Daniel and myself included, who had big aspirations for the restaurant. If we stopped in our tracks, that group was going to feel we were squandering momentum.

But we were already squandering momentum by trying to do too much too soon. We had to rebuild the engine before we could shift into fifth gear.

So I drastically cut what we were asking the dining room team to learn. It helped that I wasn't super knowledgeable about the kind of food and wine we were serving. Because I was learning the material right alongside my team, I had a better sense for what we needed to know—and for how big those pieces of information could be, while still remaining digestible.

Eventually, yes: we'd know all seven microclimates in a particular vineyard, and we'd charm guests with tales of the winemaker's grandfather and what his work in the French Resistance had to do with the enigmatic image on the label. First, though, the basics: "This is a 2005 chardonnay made by Au Bon Climat in California, aged in neutral French oak. It's bright and mineral with firm acidity, and it pairs perfectly with the Scottish salmon with daikon, baby leeks, and citrus."

We started giving the servers a food and wine test every two weeks. That probably seemed punitive to some members of the old guard, but it was part of the move toward clarity: now that we were communicating clearly what we expected people to learn, it made sense to hold them accountable.

But I outright rejected the first food and wine test the managers presented to me; it was much, much too hard. "Nobody's going to pass this! *I* wouldn't pass this." The point of these tests wasn't to fail people or to call them out; it was to make sure they felt confident and knew what they needed to know. Ultimately, this is one of a manager's biggest responsibilities: to **make sure people who are trying and working hard have what they need to succeed.**

It wasn't much longer before I finally delivered my rousing, Christopher Russell–style speech. It wasn't at my first pre-meal, or even my thirtieth, but the one I gave after I'd finally started to feel confident that everyone was talking to one another and to me and knew what was expected of them.

"We're going to make this restaurant one of the best restaurants in New York," I told the assembled team. "It's not going to be easy, because being the best is never easy, but we are going to try to make it fun. If that's not right for you, I totally get it; we'll help you find a better fit. But if the idea of working at one of the most exciting restaurants in New York gets you fired up, then I hope you stick around, because we're about to take off.

"I promise I'll try to be consistent, to do what's fair and what's right." Then I did quote Christopher: "I'm also clear about what my job is, which is to do what's best for the restaurant, not to do what's best for any of you. More often than not, what's best for the restaurant will include doing what's best for you. But the only way I can take care of all of you as individuals is by always putting the restaurant first."

I finished with my own words: "We're going to make the kind of place *we* want to eat at; we're going to create the four-star restaurant for the next generation. That's where we're going. Will you come?"

CHAPTER 8

BREAKING RULES AND BUILDING A TEAM

"Um, Will? Can I talk to you for a second?"

Apparently, I'd done something wrong. While walking through the dining room during an early service, I recognized a good regular from Tabla. It was great to see him again, and I spent a couple of minutes at the table, chatting warmly and catching up.

A few minutes later, the service director, firmly in the fine-dining faction, had caught up with me. "You leaned on the table? When you were talking to 42? That's a real fine-dining no-no. We don't put our hands on the table. We never do that." I felt for the guy: it's awkward to yell at someone when that person is also your boss.

"How come?" I wasn't trying to be a jerk; I was genuinely curious.

I thought his head was going to explode. "It's a classic rule of fine dining, that you don't touch the table."

"But why?"

"I don't know why; we just don't. *We just don't do that.*"

It was a small, awkward moment in a period full of them. But for me, it took on an outsize significance and determined my approach to how we moved forward.

Before I started at EMP, I'd done a short training at the Modern, the most formal restaurant in Danny's company at the time. It had been uncomfortable. I knew many of the people who worked there, but I'd always been the casual café guy, and they didn't bother hiding their skepticism about my new role at Eleven Madison Park. One of the senior managers went so far as to ask me, "Why do you think you're going to be able to succeed there? You've never even worked at a four-star restaurant." She wasn't being mean; given my background and stated interests, I was not a natural fit.

Over the years, though, I came to see my four-star inexperience not as a weakness but as a superpower. My inexperience enabled me to look critically at every step of service and to interrogate the only thing that mattered: the guests' experience. Did a rule bring us closer to our ultimate goal, which was connecting with people? Or did it take us further from it?

Most of the time, excellent training makes you better at what you do. Athletes practice all day every day so their muscle memory will take over as soon as the ball or the racket is in their hands. By definition, impeccable training enables you to perform your tasks without needing to think about why you're doing what you're doing—which is fantastic if your job is to have an astronomical free-throw percentage.

But muscle memory isn't always a good thing; training like that can also be like putting on a pair of blinders. Those meticulously schooled fine-dining folks were doing what they'd always done; they weren't thinking critically about the rules they were enforcing. They weren't in any position to determine whether those rules were good ones or not.

When you ask, "Why do we do it this way?" and the only answer is "Because that's how it's always been done," that rule deserves another look.

Knowing less is often an opportunity to do more. I'm no enemy of tradition—indeed, I believe much of our success at EMP was rooted in our deep love of the history of restaurants and our respect for many of the classic rituals associated with fine dining, even as we were determined to refresh the model. But a rule borne out of tradition that doesn't serve the guest—or, worse, one that stands in the way of a staff member being able to cultivate an authentic relationship with the person they are serving? That wasn't going to work.

In fact, I suspected blind faithfulness to those rules was why so many of those long-esteemed, established four-star restaurants had closed.

Tastes change. My great-grandmother wouldn't have recognized almost anything on the walls at MoMA as art; two generations later, I loved it. In the same vein, my friends and I didn't want to eat at the kind of place where the waiter stood, statue-still, next to our table with his hands clasped behind his back (and yes, I'm using that "he" deliberately). I wanted to celebrate at a restaurant where the people serving me felt comfortable enough to lean in and chat—even if it meant putting their hands on the snowy white tablecloth in front of me.

As it turned out, hands on the table was the first of many fine-dining rules we would get rid of at Eleven Madison Park.

Fairly soon, we also started to serve our soufflés "wrong." I'll spare you the technicalities, but in the classical presentation, the server turns their body away from the guest, ending up with their elbow near the guest's face. *My* way—the "wrong" way—enabled the server to maintain eye contact and a conversation with the person they were serving, which was the clear priority in my eyes.

Later, we'd have cooks run food to the tables in their whites—and they were encouraged to kneel on the ground when they spieled the dish, if they felt comfortable doing so. They hadn't done *that* at Le Pavillon.

My unorthodoxy drove the fine-dining crew nuts; how the hell were we supposed to get another star from *The New York Times* if we couldn't even get the basics right? But I wasn't suggesting you could serve a soufflé any which way; I simply wanted it done in such a way that tradition didn't interfere with hospitality.

It was a different kind of correct.

Similarly, when I first got to Eleven Madison Park, our goodbye gift was a small bag of canelés. These dark pastries, flavored with rum and vanilla and baked in special copper molds coated with butter and beeswax, are notoriously difficult to make, so the gift was one last impressive flex as the guest was on their way out the door.

To me, this seemed unnecessary. If we hadn't wowed them with everything they'd experienced over the course of their meal, then it wasn't going to happen. In the best-case scenario, those pastries would be gobbled down in the cab on the way home; at worst, the little bag would end up going stale on the kitchen counter. The canelés were too much about what *we* wanted to serve and not enough about what our guests might actually want to eat.

When you get too caught up in showing your prowess—"Look at what we can do!"—you're losing focus on the only thing that matters, which is what will make your customer happy. So we canceled the canelés and sent our guests home with a jar of granola instead. Because most people don't eat obscure French pastries for breakfast, but everyone is psyched to sit down to a bowl of granola and yogurt.

It was excellent coconut and pistachio granola, in a jar stamped with our four leaves. (The morning granola was often the last photo in a guest's Instagram post about their meal.) But it was also an intentionally humble final touch, designed to make our guests feel that, even after all the sumptuous luxury, they had been welcomed into someone's home.

In restaurants—and in all customer-service professions—the goal is to connect with people. Hospitality means breaking down barriers, not putting them up! We would spend the next ten years coming up with systemized and intentional ways to break down those barriers. Some of them were complex, but the first one was easy: Create a genuine relationship, and do what you need to in order to connect with the people you're serving.

Hire the Person, Not the Résumé

In the early days at EMP, I was at the restaurant all the time.

It was good for the people who worked for me to see I was in the trenches with them. I wouldn't hesitate before jumping in to help, whether that meant lending a hand to clear a table or attending to a disgruntled guest.

Really, though, I was there so that eventually I wouldn't have to be.

At the end of the day, it doesn't matter how good *I* am at taking care of people. This is purely a numbers game; even in a modest-size restaurant, there's no way one manager can touch every single table or connect with every guest. A leader needs to be able to trust that their team will operate on the same level as they do. Which meant that if I was going to make any kind of meaningful change, I was going to have to surround myself with a great team.

But as I set out to do that, I made the conscious decision to veer away from servers who had fine-dining experience. Our intention was to usher in a more elegant style of service, but I found if I hired people who had worked in fine dining, they already had too many bad habits. So we started looking for people with the right attitude and philosophy of hospitality.

We were looking for the kind of person who runs after a stranger on the street to return a dropped scarf, who stops by with a plate of cookies to welcome a new family to the neighborhood, or who offers to help carry a stranger's heavy stroller up the subway stairs. The kind of truly hospitable person, in other words, who wants to do good things, not for financial gain or some sort of karmic bump, but because the idea of bestowing graciousness upon others makes their own day better.

So it didn't matter if our new hires didn't know a ton about wine or how to pronounce *turbot*. If they were excited about what we were up to, then we could teach them what they needed to know.

Fairly quickly, I implemented a new policy: everyone we hired started as a kitchen server, running food from the kitchen to the dining room. This meant they started at the lowest position in the dining room, even if their previous position had been as a general manager somewhere else.

Practically speaking, this helped with the weeding process; if someone was going to balk at starting out as a kitchen server, they probably weren't a good fit. And the system helped us to train people in a way that was truly comprehensive, because what we needed them to know was much bigger than the correct way to open a bottle of wine.

It's a cliché that culture can't be taught; it has to be caught. And what better way to appreciate the exquisite nature of Daniel's food than to spend six months ferrying plates from the kitchen to the table? More important, while we were teaching people the technical points a little bit at a time, it would give them the opportunity to fully absorb the culture we were building, long before they became point person with a guest.

And how we chose which people to invite onto the team became central to our success.

Every Hire Sends a Message

You know in the movies when the soldier shouts, "Cover me," then runs across the field while his squadron protects him by raining fire on the enemy? A little dramatic for a metaphor about working in restaurants, fine—but if you don't trust the people behind you, then you're never going to perform that huge, heroic hospitality gesture (or even a tiny one) that ultimately saves the day.

When EMP was up and running, I felt confident that the entire team had my back—literally. Let's say I was clearing a table and a guest started to engage me in conversation. It's gross to stand there chatting with an armful of dirty dishes, yet I never wanted to squander an opportunity to connect with a guest. So I'd tuck the dishes behind my back, knowing that no matter how badly my wrists strained, in a second or two, one of my colleagues would notice and be on their way to grab them from me.

That's one small example, of a thousand that might happen over the course of an evening, of how a trusting team operates. And it's why hiring is such a sobering responsibility. Because when you're hiring, you're hiring not only the people who are going to represent and support you, but the people who are going to represent and support the team already working for you.

Morale is fickle, and even one individual can have an outsize and asymmetrical impact on the team, in either direction. Bring in someone who's optimistic and enthusiastic and really cares, and they can inspire those around them to care more and do better. Hire someone lazy, and it means your best team members will be punished for their excellence, picking up the slack so the overall quality doesn't drop.

At the end of the day, the best way to respect and reward the A players on your team is to surround them with other A players. This is how you attract more A players. And it means you must invest as much energy into hiring as you expect the team to invest in their jobs. You cannot expect someone to keep giving all of themselves if you put someone alongside them who isn't willing to do the same. **You need to be as unreasonable in how you build your team as you are in how you build your product or experience.**

It's also why you've got to hire slow. It's so dreadful to be shorthanded that managers tend to rush in and find a body to fill the void. I know what it's like to think, *We need someone so desperately—how bad could this person be?*

I've also (unfortunately) been in a position to find out the answer to that question. It's more detrimental to saddle yourself and your team with the wrong person, suffer the damage they do, and then end up right where you started three weeks later. Everyone would rather work a couple of extra shifts a week until you find the right person.

Someone wise once told me, "When you hire, you should ask yourself: Could this person become one of the top two or three on the team? They don't necessarily have to be all the way there yet, but they should have the potential to be."

We were gearing up for a big push. I needed to be confident that anyone could shout, "Cover me," knowing that the rest of the team would have their back.

Build a Cultural Bonfire

Many people get into restaurant work because it's a flexible, fun way to pay their bills while they devote time and energy to whatever it is they really want to do. And at the old EMP, a server could punch the clock, put in their hours, and leave work at work, which made it a great job if you were also attending art school or planning a Broadway debut.

But it was quickly becoming the kind of restaurant that required more, and the food and wine tests provided us with an efficient way to find out who was up to the challenge and who needed to move on. Some people, from both factions, understood what we were trying to do and decided they wanted to take the ride with us. Others decided they'd be happier with less of a commitment, which meant we had to replace them.

In truth, hiring was hard before we got the culture of the restaurant fully dialed in. When we had an opening, I'd find someone good to join the team—not necessarily impeccably trained, but energetic and enthusiastic about the mission. But even if that person was all charged up when they got hired, the residual negativity of some of their colleagues would eventually infect them. The fine-dining crew was still being snooty, and some of the remaining members of the old guard weren't ever going to get on board.

Three or four times, I hired someone I thought showed promise. But they'd last only a month before the flame of their enthusiasm dimmed and died, and then they'd quit.

So the next time a position opened up, I didn't race to fill it. Instead, I waited until another position came open, and then another, and then hired three great people, all at the same time. Instead of one new person cupping their hands, trying to protect the tiny flame of their enthusiasm, that little crew brought a bonfire no one could put out.

In the years to come, I would tell every group at their new-hire meeting, "You are part of a class, just as if you were starting college. Lean on one another; support one another." But the first time I ever gave that speech, it was to those three. I wanted them to know that if they approached their shared experience as a team, the impact they could have on the restaurant would be profound.

Make It Cool to Care

In high school, the cool kids tend to be the underachievers. Cool kids don't study; they don't care what the teachers think of them. At that age, it's slicker to hold back, to keep your cards close to your chest so it never looks like you're trying too hard.

Except that when you grow up a little, you realize the people getting the most out of their lives are the ones who wear their hearts on their sleeves, the ones who allow themselves to be passionate and open and vulnerable, and who approach everything they love at full-throttle, with curiosity and delight and unguarded enthusiasm.

That was my friend Brian Canlis in a nutshell.

I like to say I had two groups of friends in college. One group I played music with and partied with. The other group was Brian. He had a gecko. He loved playing chess. He wore purple Converse, and he always had a yo-yo on him. He was the complete opposite of all my other friends—and he was more confident than any of us.

Even during our first year in college, when most kids are trying to figure out who they are—and all too often pretending to be things they're not to fit in—Brian was uniquely himself. He was unapologetically invested in the things he cared about, and he never let other people's cynicism or a bad attitude distract him. His energy set the tone. Which made him the coolest person I knew, despite the fact that nothing about him was objectively cool.

We found each other on one of the first days of school and quickly discovered we'd both grown up in restaurants. In 1950, Brian's grandfather built the fine-dining restaurant Canlis, which *The New York Times* later called "Seattle's fanciest, finest restaurant for more than 60 years." His dad, Chris Canlis, ran the restaurant for thirty years before eventually turning it over to Brian and his brother Mark. (And if you want a case study of how a business can build loyalty and strengthen community in the midst of a restaurant-devastating global pandemic, check out Canlis's Instagram account for 2020.)

Restaurants aside, Brian and I could not have been more different. Nevertheless, we sat together in every class and worked together on every group project, including a truly horrendous restaurant test concept named Agave, which featured his gecko, Milo, sitting proudly atop the host stand.

I'd always been good at school, but I'd never had a partner in crime before. With Brian, I didn't have to worry about being a try-hard, an overachiever—I could go for it, engaging fully in what I was studying. Soon, my other friends started circling our little group, curious to see if we'd open our study sessions—not just because we were getting great grades, but because we were having a blast getting them.

Brian had made it cool to care.

That's why I thought of him the day I realized caring had become cool at EMP. There was a soup course we did in those early days that took three people to run for a six-top. If you did it just right, the three runners got to the table at the exact same moment, put the bowls they were holding in their left hands onto the table, moved one step to the side, switched the bowl that had been in their right hands into their left, and put that bowl down, too. Then, in glorious synchronicity, they lifted the lids from all six bowls simultaneously.

Plenty of fine-dining restaurants feature synchronized service, and most of them made sure that the plates dropped at the same time. But many times, I'd watched two runners circling the table, waiting for the third one to arrive, so that what was meant to be elegant felt awkward instead.

Not the end of the world, maybe—but not perfect, either.

For me, this was important. If we cared about this particular service detail, we should do it just right. Dancers learn choreography so their movements are precisely coordinated with the people on either side of them, and that was all this was—choreography. The runners bringing up the rear would have to move a little faster so they'd arrive at the table at the same time as their colleagues in the front, who would in turn move a little more slowly to give their buddies time to catch up. Turn, drop the first plate, step, switch, drop plate number two, lids.

We practiced it. And practiced it, and practiced it, and practiced it.

One day, I was running food with two other people on the team, and we killed it. Our delivery was so perfect you could imagine it filmed from above in one of those 1950s movies where the dancers bloom like flowers.

When we got back into the kitchen, one of the other guys turned to me, a gleeful grin on his face, and gave me the most exuberant high five I've ever gotten. We'd nailed it, and he'd gotten the same dopamine rush from it I had. We were overachievers—we cared—and we were proud of it.

The conversations I started overhearing at family meal were chang-ing, too. People were talking excitedly, not about the new bar or their most recent hookup, but about a table they'd had the night before and how happy they'd been able to make them.

They were talking about hospitality—giving and receiving it. (I was almost more excited to hear them breathlessly sharing details about the meals they'd had at other places—there's no more powerful incentive to give great hospitality than to be on the receiving end of it.) And their colleagues were hanging on every word. When you find a group that cares about the same things you care about, you don't have to hide your passions—you can sing them from the rooftops. And when the people you work with aren't hanging back but cranking it all the way up, then you can meet them there; you don't have to dim your light to succeed.

At EMP, it had become cool to care.

CHAPTER 9

WORKING WITH PURPOSE, ON PURPOSE

"THE PLACE NEEDED A BIT of Miles Davis."

I remember reading that out loud to Daniel in the windowless back office we shared. He screwed up his face and, in his heavy Swiss accent, asked me: "What the hell does that mean?"

I had no idea, but I wanted to find out.

I was reading an old review of Eleven Madison Park, written by Moira Hodgson for the *New York Observer*. The review, which had come out in April 2006—just a few months before I'd arrived at EMP, and a few months after Daniel had gotten there—was a good one. Hodgson had given the restaurant three and a half out of four stars, which might have been better than they deserved, given that they were still struggling to get food to the right tables.

But I wasn't reading that old review to find out what we could do better; I'd unearthed it because at the time we were looking for language to articulate our vision to the team. We were satisfied with our mission statement—to be the four-star restaurant for the next generation—but that was the what.

We needed the how.

Don't Try to Be All Things to All People

Speaking of reviews and criticism—I read it. All of it. Every word (with the exception of most comment sections).

I'm always interested in what others, and not just the esteemed critic from *The New York Times*, think about what we're doing. **If your business involves making people happy, then you can't be good at it if you don't care what people think.** The day you stop reading your criticism is the day you grow complacent, and irrelevance won't be far behind.

But I don't change something every time one or two people say they don't like something—maybe not even if a lot of them don't like it! If you try to be all things to all people, it's proof that you don't have a point of view—and if you want to make an impact, you need to have a point of view.

Restaurants are creative pursuits. As with most creative endeavors, there's no clear right or wrong. The choices you make are *always* going to be subjective, a matter of opinion.

What criticism offers you, then, is an invitation to have your perspective challenged—or at least to grow by truly considering it. You might stick with a choice you've been criticized for or end up somewhere completely different. The endgame isn't the point as much as the process: you grow when you engage with another perspective and decide to decide again.

Articulate Your Intentions

Unlike his fellow greats Dizzy Gillespie or Duke Ellington, who developed signature sounds and spent their careers refining them, Miles Davis reinvented himself—radically, drastically—with every consecutive album. Those reinventions often alienated fans and infuriated critics—and, equally often, went on to challenge and change modern music.

Davis's influences were incredibly eclectic and wide-ranging. He was in dialogue with rock, pop, flamenco, and classical music from the Western world, as well as with Indian and Arabic musical ideas—all while he was reinventing jazz, the quintessential American art form.

He could be difficult. He'd yell at reporters who asked stupid questions and was known for turning his back on audiences. (Side note: I did *not* look to Miles Davis when it came to inspiration for our hospitality.) And yet, Davis was also a fantastic collaborator. He went out of his way to make music with and to promote some of the most incredible musicians of the twentieth century—greats like John Coltrane, Bill Evans, Cannonball Adderley, Wayne Shorter, Red Garland, Paul Chambers, Wynton Kelly, and too many others to name. Not only did he partner freely and openly with those musicians on his work in the studio, he encouraged them to find their own voices, pursue their own projects, and thrive in their own careers.

To this day, I can't say for sure what Moira Hodgson was trying to tell us. But the more we learned about Miles and the approach he took to his work, the more inspired we became about how we wanted to approach ours. That throwaway reference turned out to be the greatest gift anyone could have given us. We had been looking for a way to put our ambitions and values into language, to find words for what we wanted to be. Researching Miles gave us eleven of them.

I had learned from my dad the importance of intentionality—knowing what it is you're trying to do, and making sure everything you do is in service of that goal. From Danny, I'd learned the importance of articulating that intention to our team.

But Daniel and I hadn't done that yet at EMP. The two of us had spent hours together, talking and planning and dreaming; we were fundamentally aligned in an intuitive way. Still, a hundred and fifty people worked for us at EMP, and every one of them had to be aligned with the mission. We needed language. **Language is how you give intention to**

your intuition and how you share your vision with others. Language is how you create a culture.

It was lucky the Hodgson review referenced a musician, because I love music and have played it my whole life. After the review, I started listening to more Miles Davis, both inside the restaurant and out. Once I was more familiar with his music, I read everything I could find about Miles and about his creative process—specifically what other musicians said about the approach he took to making music and how that process resulted in the enormous impact he had on the form.

Over the next month or two, I worked with the team to create a list of the words that came up over and over again when critics and other musicians talked about Miles:

> Cool
> Endless Reinvention
> Inspired
> Forward Moving
> Fresh
> Collaborative
> Spontaneous
> Vibrant
> Adventurous
> Light
> Innovative

These resonated with us and became a road map of sorts. (The list was long, but we wanted eleven.) The review had been right: if our restaurant was going to evolve, it *did* need more Miles Davis.

We printed a large sign with those words underneath our logo and hung it in our kitchen. That sign became a touchstone, a guiding light, a way to hold ourselves accountable. Whenever we were brainstorming or facing a difficult decision, we looked at the list. The restaurant would change radically over the years that followed, but we felt confident that what we were doing would make sense, as long as we stayed true to the words on that list.

"Cool" was the first word on the list. That seemed right, as we'd already articulated the importance of that concept for ourselves: if we were going to create a four-star restaurant for the next generation, it was going to have to be cool.

In the years to come, many would say "endless reinvention" was the defining characteristic of our restaurant, which did change, over and over again—not ever for the sake of change itself but because in order to be the best in the world, we had to be authentic. For us, that meant serving to others what we wished to receive, and as we grew and matured and evolved, what *we* wanted to receive changed, and so did what we served to others.

But of all the words on that list, "collaborative" was the one we seized on as the first one to pursue. It stood out to us, almost as if it had been highlighted: the one word that would provide us with the key to all the others on the list.

Strategy Is for Everyone

The fact we'd found fundamental inspiration from a restaurant critic pointing to a jazz trumpeter gave us the idea there might be merit in looking for guidance in other, unexpected places—especially those outside the metaphorical walls of the restaurant world.

When companies expand, they often say, "The bigger we get, the smaller we have to act." (This was a mantra at Shake Shack.) At EMP in the early days, we went the other way. We were a single restaurant—part of a bigger company, but operated as if we weren't, with a huge amount of autonomy. We were little, but we wanted to act big.

We looked at organizations known for extraordinary company cultures—huge companies, like Nordstrom and Apple and JetBlue. They all held strategic planning sessions, or long-form meetings where groups from across the organization got together to brainstorm ways for the company to grow. (Very corporate-smart.)

This was a revelation to us; the practice is still virtually unheard of in the restaurant world. It was also a relief. Up until then, Daniel and I had been doing all the decision-making and goal-setting by ourselves. Why, when we'd assembled a crew of vibrant, bright young people who loved restaurants and food and hospitality? No matter how ambitious or innovative we were, we could never hope to match the combined brainpower of our entire staff.

Immediately we could see how inviting our team to take part in identifying and naming the goals of the company would increase the likelihood we'd all meet those goals together. Of course we'd be able to come up with more (and better!) ideas if they were involved—not to mention the sense of ownership they'd get from making those contributions.

Over time, our strategic planning meetings became brainstorming sessions, where we'd decide as a collective what we wanted to do in the year to come. But that first year, we posed only one question: What do we want to embody?

We wanted to be one of the best restaurants in New York. We wanted to make our restaurant excellent without sacrificing warmth, contemporary without compromising standards. But before we set out on that journey, we needed to know how we characterized ourselves, both as individuals and as a team.

Our first-ever strategic planning meeting took place in 2007. We closed the restaurant for the day—admittedly unreasonable—and invited everyone who worked at EMP to come together and strategize as a team about our future.

This inclusivity was important. At many of the companies we'd studied, strategic planning was reserved for upper management, but we included everybody on the team, from the assistant general manager and the chef de cuisine all the way to the dishwashers, prep cooks, and assistant servers, which is what we called our bussers.

We were lucky we were small enough for that to be possible, because a busser sees all kinds of things a general manager never can. If we were serious about every detail, then everyone's perspective and vantage point would be valuable.

On the day itself, I introduced the concept of the meeting, explained what we hoped to get out of it—and got out of the team's way.

They broke into ten groups, scattered across the restaurant, each gathered around a notebook. I spent the day walking from group to group, noting as people got excited, argued, and laughed with one another. I dropped in but was careful not to contribute. This was their time.

Because I didn't want anyone to feel that they couldn't speak freely, we'd had the dining room and kitchen managers do their strategic planning the day before. On the day of the team meeting, managers had a different role: the sous-chefs came out into the dining room and took custom sandwich orders from the staff, while the dining room managers staffed the kitchen, putting the orders together. (Give people a safe space to mess with their bosses, and some of them are going to go for it—I remember one request for a turkey sandwich featuring one slice of untoasted wheat, one slice of toasted rye, and three dots of mayo.) These two groups switching roles left everyone with a new appreciation for the difficulties their counterparts faced every night.

In the afternoon, the ten groups stood up to present what they'd come up with, and we saw how aligned we were. Ultimately, four words took center stage. None of them were particularly groundbreaking on their own, but we determined they could be—if we could embody all of them simultaneously.

> Education
> Passion
> Excellence
> Hospitality

Education was a no-brainer. We had always known that we wanted to build a culture based on teaching and learning, and to hire those who were curious about what they didn't know and generous with what they did. Similarly, we wanted people who were passionate about the mission, as fired up as we were about what we were trying to accomplish.

But it was the two remaining words on the list—and the inherent conflict between them—that would inform everything we did going forward.

Choose Conflicting Goals

Hospitality and excellence. Those two concepts? They're not friends.

It's easy to have a sweet culture of hospitality if you're not going to be maniacal about precision and detail. Who cares if the waitress at the diner forgot to bring your Coke? What's a little sloppiness between friends?

And it's pretty easy to scare your staff so they almost never, ever make a technical misstep in the dining room. But, all ethical objections aside, if they're living in constant fear of being caught in a mistake, you're not going to get their most realized, relaxed selves interacting with your guests.

In fact, I could hear the tension between these two concepts when I was walking around that first strategic planning meeting. Some people were arguing passionately about the importance of welcome and warmth and connection, while others were convinced nothing should take precedence over an impeccably trained staff and spit-polishing every formal aspect of the restaurant to a perfect shine.

Putting both hospitality and excellence on our list was a way of recognizing that success was going to come from approaching the problem of hospitality vs. excellence in the most difficult way possible: in order to succeed, we needed to be good at both. This wasn't an either/or—it was an and. Later, I would learn that the management guru Roger Martin calls this "integrative thinking." In *When More Is Not Better*, he argues that leaders should actually go out of their way to choose conflicting goals.

Southwest Airlines, for instance, set out to be both the lowest-cost airline in America *and* number one in both customer and employee satisfaction. Those goals would seem to be in opposition, and perhaps they are. But much of the time, they've succeeded at all three. Certainly, the efforts they've made toward those contradictory goals have done wonders for their bottom line: for the last half century, Southwest has been the most profitable airline in the country.

As Martin says, multiple conflicting goals force you to innovate. We'd seen it ourselves. When I'd arrived at EMP, one faction had been sacrificing hospitality in the name of precision and excellence, while the other had been delivering warmer service with less finesse. Those who survived and thrived with us had been able to see the merit in the other group's priorities.

By putting both words on our list, we were acknowledging that we would need to recognize the inherent friction between hospitality and excellence. We would need to explore that contradiction and embrace it—integrating two opposing ideas and embodying both simultaneously.

Know Why Your Work Is Important

When I was coming up in hospitality, it was pretty common for parents to lament their children's decision to pursue a career in restaurants. They wanted their kids to be doctors, or lawyers, or bankers; they didn't want them to serve other people—and especially not as a career.

I had a different point of view. I wanted our team members to understand that hospitality elevates service not only for the person receiving it, but for the person delivering it. Serving other human beings can feel demeaning, unless you first stop and acknowledge the importance of the work and the impact you can have on others when you're doing it.

I wrapped up that first strategic planning meeting by telling the team, "The moment you start to pursue service through the lens of hospitality, you understand there's nobility in it. We may not be saving people's lives, but we do have the ability to make their lives better by creating a magical world they can escape to—and I see that not as an opportunity, but as a responsibility, and a reason for pride."

I took a call recently from a Cornell hotel-school grad looking for career advice. The first thing he said was, "I'm trying to figure out whether or not I want to stay in this horrible industry." It was a short call; I told him pretty quickly it sounded like he shouldn't.

No matter what you do, it's hard to excel if you don't love it. I've had bad days and weeks like everyone else, but I've always been able to say, "I can't imagine doing anything else," because I've always been able to tap into what's important about my job. I genuinely believe that in restaurants we can give people a break from reality even just for a short time—and, as cheesy as it sounds, that we can make the world a better place. Because when you're really, really nice to people, they'll be really nice to others, who will in turn pay it forward. That energizes me, even when I'm depleted.

I've made it my mission to help the people who work for me see what's important about what they do. Even at MoMA, we didn't see our guests as a bunch of customers looking for lunch; we saw them as museumgoers—people on an adventure, realizing their dream of being inspired at one of the greatest modern art museums on earth. That simple shift had an automatic and profound impact on how our team acted, and on the hospitality our guests received.

I speak to people across industries and in different fields. When I encounter someone who thinks their work doesn't matter, it's usually because they haven't dug deep enough to recognize the importance of the role they play. When I spoke at a real estate conference, it was easy for me to tell when someone was operating with passion and purpose. Many told me they sold houses; the great ones understood they were selling homes.

This applies to every industry I can think of. You can be in the financial services business, or in the business of providing people with a plan so they can provide a future for their families. You can be in the insurance business, or in the business of offering people the comfort of knowing they and their loved ones are covered, safe and secure, no matter what happens. It's the difference between coming to work to do a job and coming to work to be a part of something bigger than yourself.

Without exception, no matter what you do, you can make a difference in someone's life. **You *must* be able to name for yourself why your work matters.** And if you're a leader, you need to encourage everyone on your team to do the same.

CHAPTER 10

CREATING A CULTURE OF COLLABORATION

THE DAY AFTER THE STRATEGIC planning meeting, the air in the restaurant was charged with promise and excitement—and that energy showed no signs of dissipating in the weeks that followed. Our passionate and creative team had a say in where the restaurant was going and were willing to work even harder because they had a stake.

We'd gotten so much out of that single day; I couldn't wait to implement more consistent and creative ways to build collaboration more fully into our culture. We'd struck gold, and I was unabashedly greedy for more.

I wanted collaboration to mean *everyone*, every single day.

Choose Worthy Rivals

In *The Infinite Game*, Simon Sinek writes about choosing a worthy rival: another company that does one or more things better than you, whose strengths reveal your weaknesses and set you on a path of constant improvement.

When I read that, I thought immediately of a dinner Daniel and I had at Per Se in late 2006—or, more specifically, of my nightcap afterward.

Before marriage and the birth of my daughter, I ended most nights in my apartment with a glass of wine and an open notebook. Those journaling sessions—part diary, part mea culpa, part vision board, part to-do list—were where my most inspired ideas came from.

Daniel and I spent a lot of time studying other, more established and successful fine-dining restaurants. What were they doing better than what we were doing? What could we learn? What could we borrow and make our own?

And in New York City, Per Se was the best of the best.

I'd been to Thomas Keller's celebrated California restaurant the French Laundry with a girlfriend years before, and I counted it—along with that first dinner at the Four Seasons and the meal with my dad in the Skybox in Daniel Boulud's kitchen—as one of the most memorable restaurant experiences of my life. I wasn't even interested in fine dining at the time, but our meal there was so extraordinary, it transcended all my hesitations. The whole experience was so freaking *excellent*, in every way, it felt entirely new.

The French Laundry is one of the best restaurants in the world, so nobody was surprised when Keller's New York debut instantly became a standard-bearer of fine-dining excellence. While EMP was far from being in Per Se's league, Daniel and I were paying close attention to every single thing they did.

So after that dinner at Per Se, I was feverishly taking notes on our experience, which had been spectacular.

Every course had been an inspiration. I loved the playfulness of the famous salmon tartare cornet, a nod to a child's ice-cream cone, and was swept away by the luxuriousness of the presentations, including a cascade of custom-made porcelain plates in ascending sizes. And I was struck by the effortless way Thomas Keller seemed able to elevate a humble idea, like coffee and donuts, into an opulent surprise.

The precision behind all that elegance was not lost on us. A small example: we'd been invited on a tour of the kitchen, filled with state-of-the-art equipment and so meticulous and beautifully designed I thought Daniel might burst into tears. While we were walking through, we noticed that the blue tape used to secure a tablecloth to the pass wasn't torn, but neatly cut with scissors. The attention, to every nearly invisible detail, filled us with awe.

Then, at the end of our meal, when we were already stupefied with delight, a showstopper: our server presented us with a board of twenty-four different chocolate truffles in three rows—dark, milk, and white—and conversationally ran through a detailed description of *every single one of them*. It was a feat of memory so audacious, so superhuman, it might as well have been a magic trick.

I scribbled frantically. Finally, I got to the cup of filter coffee I'd been served after dinner. It was a perfectly fine cup of coffee, but because everything else about that meal had been so unbelievably *perfect* perfect, that just-okay cup of coffee stood out.

And it made me think about Jim Betz.

Tap in to Their Passions—Then Give Them the Keys

Jim Betz was an unrepentant coffee geek who worked with me at EMP.

I'd gotten into coffee a little bit when I was running the cafés at MoMA and was lucky enough to live around the corner from Ninth Street Espresso, one of the first serious espresso bars in the city. The owner, Ken Nye, was notoriously exacting: he would adjust the coarseness of the grind throughout the day in response to the humidity outside, and toss any shot he felt wasn't up to snuff.

Jim was Ken's nephew, as passionate and knowledgeable as his uncle. He was also deeply committed to our restaurant. He'd shown up for his interview with a huge, Williamsburg-hipster, lumberjack-style beard, which

I told him he'd have to shave off if he wanted the job. He arrived the next day with a naked chin, for the first time in years; I don't know if there's a greater sign of commitment.

Jim was much (much) more knowledgeable on the subject of coffee than I was, but I knew just enough to be fun for him to talk to, and the two of us would often find each other at family meal to chat about a new shop with high standards or some excellent beans we'd tried. Though Jim was only in his early twenties, I learned from him whenever we compared notes. So I couldn't help but anticipate his disappointment when I told him about that just-okay cup of coffee at Per Se.

The truth is that while that "perfectly fine" cup of coffee was somewhat shocking in the context of our otherwise extraordinary meal, it was pretty unsurprising, given the state of coffee service at fine-dining restaurants at the time.

You went to those restaurants expecting incredible food and amazing wine. Those were expected: table stakes, the price of admission. The ancillary programs, though—the cocktail to start your meal, the cup of tea or coffee at the end—were mediocre. And this remained true, even though there had been a complete revolution in those areas outside those hallowed walls.

It had been a long time, for instance, since beer had meant the pale, flavorless industrial lager that dominated the commercial market in the 1950s. Thousands of small, independent breweries all over the world were creating beers with complex flavors that could more than stand up to excellent food. So maybe there'd been no such thing as a beer pairing at a four-star restaurant in the eighties—but by 2006, it should have been inconceivable to imagine a four-star restaurant for the next generation without one.

The same was true for cocktails: if most people who cared about food knew that a proper Manhattan should be stirred, not shaken, why were so many places still making airport-lounge-quality drinks? And why would a thousand-dollar meal end with generic, machine-filtered coffee, when I could stop and have a glorious, high-grade, single-origin shot pulled by a professional barista at a hole-in-the-wall like Ninth Street on my way in to work?

These programs lagged because nobody was paying attention to them. Even today, in most fine-dining restaurants, the person running all the beverage programs is the wine director. That person is, by definition, fanatical about wine and has devoted their life to studying it; the majority of their travel, reading, and professional education has been in wine—not beer, or espresso, or cocktails, or tea.

This was true even if your wine director was one of the best in the world—and I knew that because the wine director at EMP, John Ragan, *was* one of the best in the world. A wine director didn't have the time to become a real expert in these other beverages, while also curating a wine list for one of the city's best restaurants.

My team, on the other hand, was crowded with young people who were wildly enthusiastic about various aspects of food and drink. A crew of them would take the train to Queens on their days off to visit outdoor beer gardens with sixty obscure microbrews on tap. Another routinely disappeared into a nondescript office building in Midtown to taste flights of first-flush gyokuro—green tea grown in the shade and prepared with water a full sixty degrees below boiling. And of course, there was Jim, waxing encyclopedic about ethical coffee-growing regions and precision-pour kettles.

Passion was one of the core values we'd committed to pursuing during our strategic planning meeting. And so the last thing I wrote in my journal after that epic dinner at Per Se was: "Jim should be in charge of our coffee program."

With that, the ownership program at Eleven Madison Park was born.

Kirk Kelewae was a Cornell grad who had joined the company all revved up about what we were doing. He was clearly going places, but, like every new hire, he started as a kitchen server, running plates of food from the kitchen to the dining room.

Kirk also happened to be wild about beer, and I was sure he'd be the perfect steward of our program, but when I first sat down with him, he was skittish—as most twenty-two-year-olds would be—about the responsibility until I convinced him we'd be there for him, every step of the way.

We introduced him to all our vendors, knowing he would soon introduce us to new ones. I came to love watching beer distributors arrive in the dining room, expecting to give the Eleven Madison Park wine director a taste of some sensational new brew, only to find themselves sitting across from a baby-faced food runner, only recently able to legally order a drink himself.

We gave Kirk a budget and showed him how to manage it. He learned how to do inventory and how to order. Then we told him: "It's yours now. Go make it awesome."

He didn't need to be told twice. He attacked every aspect of our beer service—from how we stored the bottles, to the glassware we used, to the technique we used to pour it. He read every trade publication and hunted down the most rare and obscure beers. All this extra work was driven by his own passion, and his youthful eagerness enchanted producers, who'd find ways to sneak him a couple of highly allocated bottles they'd made only a few dozen of.

I was thrilled but not overly surprised when, a year into Kirk's reign, Eleven Madison Park was listed as one of the best beer programs in America in a number of different publications.

Not only did our beer program improve exponentially, but Kirk's fervor was contagious; we all caught the beer bug because nobody wanted to let him down. He'd pour tastes and chase you down in the hallways: "Hey—you've got to taste this gruit!" (Know what that is? Neither did I. Thanks to Kirk, I can now tell you that it's a medieval-style beer brewed using bitter botanicals instead of hops. Apparently, it's a thing.)

Similarly, Sambath Seng, another food runner, took over our tea program. She flew to Las Vegas to attend the World Tea Expo and introduced herself to distributors who were buying tea directly from gardens in India and China and Thailand and Taiwan and Korea and Japan. She taught us about teas that had been roasted, as well as others processed with steam. Because she cared deeply about water purity, precisely calibrated brewing times and temperature combinations, and how proper teaware should be warmed and handled, we cared, too.

Cocktails were next. I got our bar team together and said, "I want to have a cocktail program as good as PDT." PDT was a cocktail bar in the East Village, run by my friend Jim Meehan. The initials stood for Please Don't Tell, a reference to the tiny bar's covert location, which you accessed, speakeasy-style, through a phone booth in Crif Dogs, a hole-in-the-wall hot dog joint. It was widely recognized as one of the best bars in the world.

One of our bartenders said, "That's ridiculous; it's not possible." It could take a bartender at the high-end cocktail bars ten full minutes to make a drink. That type of service would be difficult to mimic in a restaurant setting, with a hundred and forty seats to serve, not six.

But as anyone who's worked for me will tell you, "We can't" is not my favorite phrase. I come by this honestly. In a particular season of my youth, I made the mistake of telling my dad about something I couldn't do. The next morning, the house was covered in printed, fortune-cookie-size pieces of paper: "Success comes in cans; failure comes in can'ts." I never said it in front of him again.

I also had a lot of faith in the guy I was talking to. His name was Leo Robitschek. Maybe you've heard of him—he's one of the foremost mixologists in the world now. But at the time, he was working at EMP while putting himself through medical school.

Leo had always been full of great ideas, but he was also the squeakiest wheel, the person on the staff who never failed to let you know why what you were doing was fundamentally flawed and never going to work. He completely transformed once given an ownership role, as if he hadn't wanted to commit to greatness until he was in charge. At the helm, he went from being our most outspoken in-house critic to a true ambassador for the restaurant—and an absolute guru in the world of quality cocktails.

Then, of course, there was Jim. In charge of coffee, he immediately switched our supplier to Intelligentsia, one of the best roasters at the time. He started making coffee tableside, giving our guests a choice between a classic Chemex pour-over or a vacuum-pot siphon system, which combined the best attributes of the immersion and filter methods and had the added benefit of being thrilling to watch in action.

Thanks to Jim (and, indirectly, to Per Se), an after-dinner cup of coffee at EMP went from being a just-fine, bulk-ordered afterthought to a highly entertaining, exquisitely crafted, educational, and theatrical experience. Most important, you ended up with a damn fine cup of coffee.

Find the Win/Win/Win

Steve Ells, the founder of Chipotle, spoke eloquently at the Welcome Conference about the positive impact of giving his team more responsibility.

Most fast-food companies process ingredients at a plant because they don't trust the teams at the stores to do it; unsurprisingly, the food arrives tasting like it's been on a truck for a couple of days. Ells believed that, with proper training, his in-house employees could make better, fresher food.

He discovered that when he gave the teams responsibility, they became *more* responsible; elevated by his trust in them, they stepped up into the role. The team was empowered, the food tasted better, and customers felt better about the food they were eating because they could see living human beings chopping tomatoes and grilling chicken.

It was a win/win/win.

It was for us, too. Our staff loved the ownership programs. Because every single person who worked for us started as a food runner, some of them could work there for three years before they became a captain. These ownership programs gave these motivated, creative people a project to engage with while they earned their stripes.

And the investment of time and trust and education was almost always worth it, because when we mentored someone into full ownership, our jobs became easier over the long term. When Leo was handling cocktails and Kirk was taking care of beer, our wine director, John Ragan, didn't need to think about those beverages or about coffee or tea. Our already stellar wine program got better because John had more time and energy and capacity to devote to it, while all those other programs, so inherently mediocre at so many other fine-dining restaurants, became absolutely best in class.

And everyone in the restaurant, whether they were working or eating there, benefited from the wonderful alchemy that comes when fervor has the room to run. Kirk eventually became close with Garrett Oliver, the mad genius who runs Brooklyn Brewery. So when Leo, through his friendship with Julian Van Winkle, got an empty Pappy barrel from the legendary Kentucky distillery, we shipped it to Brooklyn Brewery, and Garrett aged a custom beer for us in it. It was an extraordinary outcome—a genuinely special, playful collaboration that would never have come about if our wine director had stayed in charge of the beer program.

When we saw what a tremendous success we were having with the beverage programs, our management team came up with a list of every aspect of the restaurant that could benefit from some attention, including linens, side work, and educational training. These were less shiny, but they would make a real difference in the experience of those who worked there, and on our bottom line.

An example: the guy who took over CGS (which stands for "china, glass, and silver"—sexy as it gets, right?) dedicated himself to reducing breakage. He discovered the racks in the dish room were half an inch too short, so the stems poked up above the top when the glasses went through the dishwasher. A couple of new glass racks later, and he'd eliminated loss by 30 percent. That's serious money, and a major morale booster, as it also meant that we no longer ran out of water glasses in the middle of service.

Then he sent the handyman out for thick rubber matting, installed it on the stainless steel table that held plates waiting to be washed, and bingo—no more chips on the raised rim at the bottom of our expensive, handmade ceramic chargers, either.

These weren't line items lost on a manager's to-do list, crowded with a thousand other things, but minor, inexpensive fixes implemented by a young person paying close attention. These small shifts saved the restaurant thousands of dollars in the first couple of months. And while some of these programs affected the guests more directly than others, you didn't have to know what the linen closet or the glass racks looked like to feel the effects.

We didn't assign these ownership programs; participation was strictly on a volunteer basis. And while many who stepped up happened to be knowledgeable about the area they'd chosen, they didn't need to start out an expert. All we asked was that they be interested and curious and have the first inklings of a passion.

"It Might Not Work" Is a Terrible Reason Not to Try

I'm not going to lie: it's much easier to not share ownership—at least to start. (This is the "It's quicker to do it myself" problem.) But refusing to delegate because it might take too long to train someone will only get in the way of your own growth.

At the beginning, the young people running these ownership programs did require tons of oversight and encouragement and advice. Mentoring them was a lot of work. And there *were* bumps in the road. Yes, we'd set up guardrails so Kirk couldn't lose a million bucks in beer, but a kid right out of hotel school is naturally going to make more mistakes than someone with ten years of experience running a beverage program.

And while it does take more time to fix someone else's mistake than to do it yourself in the first place, these are short-term investments of time with long-term gains. If you insist on a manager having previous managerial experience, you'll never be able to promote a promising server into the role. By definition, then, it's impossible to promote from within if you wait until an employee has all the experience they need. **Often, the perfect moment to give someone more responsibility is *before* they're ready.** Take a chance, and that person will almost always work extra hard to prove you right. Given that I eventually promoted Kirk to the position of general manager of EMP—you could say the investment paid off.

While I'm being candid, there's another reason it's easier not to do this: it might not work. We learned the hard way, for instance, that it was best if the person running the linen program was a hardheaded organizational dynamo who could stay on top of inventory, manage expenses, and take pleasure in maintaining a tidy, operationally efficient closet— not a visionary dreamer.

But if we were trying to encourage people to take a shot, we couldn't penalize them if they didn't succeed; we simply found another area where they could invest their time. It's always been my belief that "It might not work" is a terrible reason not to try an idea, especially one that has the potential upside of making the people who work for you more engaged with your mission.

The Best Way to Learn Is to Teach

My dad says that the best way to learn is to teach, and he taught me to study for tests as if I were going in to deliver a presentation. I found that if I studied the material as if I was going to have to turn around and teach it, I learned it much more thoroughly than I would have otherwise.

At EMP, I made teaching part of our culture.

The spirit of collaboration that came out of the ownership program was inspiring to all of us, but asking someone to take over an entire department was an enormous commitment. So when John Ragan began a weekly meeting called Happy Hour, dedicated to the wine, beer, and cocktails on our menu, we encouraged the team to step in and give presentations of their own.

A onetime presentation was much less of an obligation than taking over an ownership program—and it was fun, because the people who worked for us *loved* food and wine. Whether they'd had a lightbulb moment with a glass of Burgundy at a wine bar and wanted to know more about the history of the region or had finally tasted a sherry that wasn't like sneaking a sip at their grandmother's bridge game, presenting at Happy Hour was an excuse to do research, then share what they'd learned with the team.

Quickly, Happy Hour topics began to transcend wine and spirits. Madison Square Park was right outside our enormous windows; one of the servers did a presentation on the storied history of the park, so we'd have interesting factoids to share with guests. (The rules of baseball were created there; the torch from the Statue of Liberty was displayed there; and it was the site of the country's first community Christmas tree lighting in 1912.) That led us to reach out to Kenneth T. Jackson, a professor at Columbia and the world's foremost authority on New York history, who gave the entire team a tour of the park and the surrounding blocks.

Jeff Taylor was our resident restaurant-history buff. Once a month, he'd do a deep dive on an iconic, old-school restaurant like Le Pavillon, which debuted at the 1939 World's Fair, launched chefs like Jacques Pépin, and defined both French food and fine dining for New Yorkers in the second half of the twentieth century.

Billy Peelle, a food runner, immersed himself in the New York Public Library's vast historic menu archive, ending up with a knockout presentation on menu design and its evolution over the second part of the twentieth century and into the twenty-first. Menu design was entirely outside the scope of Billy's role; it was a project I handled myself, in collaboration with our graphic designer. But he knew his presentation would connect us to our heritage—the legacy we had charged ourselves with defending and extending. Perhaps it's not a surprise that, years later, Billy also went on to be the general manager.

Let Them Lead

Those Happy Hours had an important side benefit. Normally, classes in a restaurant are led by the managers, not the staff, but as more and more members of the hourly team led classes, they acted more like leaders.

I wanted to push this one step further.

I've already said I believe the most important moment of leadership each day in a restaurant is the pre-meal meeting, when the manager steps out to teach and inspire and get the team aligned before service. Once a week on Saturdays, we took the responsibility of leading that meeting away from the managers and gave it to a member of the team.

Leading pre-meal meant acting as emcee, following the template I'd established: basic internal housekeeping about stuff like paychecks and health insurance, then a short speech about a service experience you'd had that you'd found exciting or inspirational. At the end, you'd hand the meeting over to a sommelier or to a sous-chef to talk about wine list and menu changes.

Of course, that middle bit was the challenge, especially if you were nervous about speaking to a group. Many people told stories about tables they'd served at EMP or service experiences they'd had elsewhere, both good and bad. You could also talk about an adventure you'd had outside the realm of food and restaurants, like the shot after my haircut. As long as the experience had taught you a lesson about making people feel seen and welcomed and appreciated, it was fair game.

Leading Saturday pre-meal gave our hourly employees the chance to step into a role ordinarily filled by managers. They were contributing not only to the education of the team, but to their inspiration. And asking the team to run these meetings and present at Happy Hour had yet another unexpected benefit: everyone became more comfortable with public speaking.

I've always been comfortable talking to a group; in high school, I did theater and student government. But, in keeping with my dad's advice to build my strengths as well as my weaknesses, I took a public speaking class at Cornell. It had a lasting impact on me and was where I learned one of the most important tenets of public speaking, which I follow to this day: Tell them what you're going to tell them, tell them, then tell them what you've told them.

The other important takeaway from that class was that **public speaking is a leadership skill**. Being able to communicate your own excitement is a powerful way to engage the people who work for and with you, and to infect them with energy and a sense of purpose.

We saw an enormous difference in the team in the months after they started leading Happy Hours and Saturday pre-meals. I loved the way they talked to guests: after all, taking an order, helping a guest make a decision about wine, or spieling a course are all forms of public speaking. They had more authority when giving instructions to their colleagues during service, too.

But the real shift was intangible; they began carrying themselves differently.

Make It Mandatory

"Mandatory" is a dirty word in the workplace these days.

Leaders tend to make enriching programs voluntary because we assume that everyone's going to be as excited about them as we are. But getting people to change their behavior is hard; sometimes you need to give them a taste of what it feels like to get them hooked.

This doesn't mean being exploitative—pay people for their time. But don't be afraid to make participation in a program mandatory.

There were lots of structured opportunities available for those who wanted to collaborate at EMP. But some people need to contribute to know how good it feels when they do, so I developed some tricks to prime the pump. One of them was to make collaboration mandatory for some of our new hires.

At every restaurant I've ever worked at, the reservations office has been a dump. The dining room looks perfect, and the kitchen must be pristine. The manager's office is usually pretty organized, or else you won't be able to find what you need when you need it, and it's good to keep the locker rooms tidy and clean, because those spaces are important for the morale of the team.

So anything without a home that needs to be moved out of the dining room gets stuffed into the reservationist's office. Promotional glasses from a liquor distributor? An extra box of Christmas decorations? A cookbook the team is passing around? It's all piled up in the reservationist's office, the restaurant equivalent of a junk drawer. And every one of them has a neglected, disorganized bulletin board, weighed down by outdated announcements and reminders.

The best way to introduce a new employee to your culture is to have them work side by side with someone who believes in it. But reservationists tend to work alone or with one other person, and they had to watch the phones instead of attending pre-meal, so they were always a little out of the cultural loop. And yet, because they were the first person guests interacted with, we wanted them to be good ambassadors.

So we used an act of mandatory collaboration to bring them into the fold. When a new reservationist was hired at Eleven Madison Park, we asked them right away to do one thing to make the reservationist's office better. This was a mandate, not an invite, though they could decide what to do and how big or small.

We had to show them, right off the bat, that we meant it when we said collaboration was welcome. Otherwise, even a real self-starter might hesitate before jumping in: *I wonder whose toes I'd be stepping on if I were to fix that nightmare of a bulletin board.*

The program was helpful, to them and for us. New people had the gift of fresh eyes and could see all the warts the rest of us had long stopped seeing.

It also helped them to break the ice with their new colleagues; we wanted people to be comfortable asking for help or clarification, and assigning a collaboration kick-started that: "Would an additional bulletin board be helpful in here? If so, who do I talk to about petty cash?" Not to mention that the inevitable thanks—"How did we live like that for so long?"—would be coming from the person's new colleagues, as well as from their boss.

Assigning a collaboration runs counter to the "Don't cannonball" advice I usually gave young managers, I know, but there's an important difference: a reservationist is an entry-level position. A lot of good comes from empowering the most junior staff.

Once people had gotten a feel for how good it felt to make a contribution, they would start actively looking for a way to do it again. And it was a way for us to communicate, on a person's very first day: *We hired you for a reason. We know you have something to contribute, and we don't want to wait to see what it is.*

Listen to Every Idea

When you spend this much time encouraging your team to contribute, you'd better make sure your team knows that your doors are always open to ideas. There's a better way to do everything, and I made it clear: if you had an idea for how we could improve, I wanted to hear it.

The first time someone comes to you with an idea, listen closely, because how you handle it will dictate how they choose to contribute in the future. Dismiss them that first time, and you'll extinguish a flame that's difficult to rekindle.

Someone may approach you with an idea you've heard before, or one you've already tried; don't automatically reject these. Maybe they've thought it through in a way you didn't previously, or circumstances have changed and you're no longer too far in front of the curve for it to work.

Someone may even come to you with an idea that's just plain dumb. That's an opportunity to teach—to listen, and then to explain in a respectful way why the idea is unlikely to work, so that the person leaves both encouraged and educated. Remember: there's often a brilliant idea right behind a bad one.

Great Leaders Create Leaders

Managers weren't always thrilled by this emphasis on collaboration, especially if they'd worked their way up through the ranks. This can be a problem in "promote from within" cultures; with power comes increased responsibility, and relinquishing those responsibilities—especially if they're new and hard-won—can feel like a demotion.

So we reminded them: great leaders make leaders. **You don't want to have a hundred keys; you win when you end up with only one—the key to the front door.** Once they'd turned over some of these responsibilities, they'd have more time to make their own contributions.

I can't overstate how much credit I give this more collaborative approach for our ultimate success: in my eyes, collaboration is the foundation upon which Unreasonable Hospitality was built. Every single program improved by leaps and bounds, in ways that surprised us. The ideas we were fielding were newer and fresher; in fact, many of the ideas we would be most celebrated for were born in those programs. And there were more of them because it wasn't only me and Daniel and a few managers coming up with a plan.

Giving the team more responsibility than they expected had an amazing impact—the more responsibility we trusted them with, the more responsible they became. The more they taught, the more they understood the importance of everything we were asking them to learn. The more they led meetings like pre-meal and Happy Hour, the more they started acting like leaders. The more practice they had with public speaking, the more confidently they carried themselves.

And because every single person on the team knew that the vision was created collectively, we were all willing to work even harder to achieve our goals.

CHAPTER 11

PUSHING TOWARD EXCELLENCE

"Will! I'm pretty sure I just sat Frank Bruni."

It was late 2006 when our breathless, wide-eyed maître d' caught up with me at the service station to tell me the food critic for *The New York Times* had just walked into the restaurant. The *Times* generally allows a few years to pass between reviews, and we weren't anywhere near due. But the hiring of an exciting new chef can sometimes trigger a re-review, and we'd been hoping that our hard work, not to mention the buzz it was creating, would inspire him to give us another look.

If Bruni was in the restaurant, our review season had begun.

To say that our team had been laser-focused on what the *Times* would have to say about the changes we'd made at Eleven Madison Park is an understatement. "Obsessed" is probably a better word.

In fairness, the stakes were high. Eleven Madison Park was, to put it bluntly, the kind of Danny Meyer restaurant that was meant to have three stars. Union Square Cafe had three stars. Gramercy Tavern had three stars. Tabla had three stars.

But EMP had gotten two stars from the *Times* when it opened, and again when it was re-reviewed in February 2005. That last, ho-hum two-star review had been the catalyst for Daniel's hiring, and for mine. So while the two of us may have been dreaming about four stars down the line, for the sake of our immediate job security—to say nothing of our sanity—we *needed* three.

It was go time.

Excellence Is the Culmination of Thousands of Details Executed Perfectly

Confession: I'm a perfectionist.

If my wife parks the car crooked, I'll repark it; if she leaves a book slightly askew on her nightstand, I'll adjust it so it lines up with the edge. Every time she makes the bed, I remake it. (Luckily, she has a good sense of humor about all this.) I can't help but see these imperfections, and it's nearly impossible to stop myself from fixing them. In order to feel at peace, I need things around me to be just right—unreasonably organized, and in their proper place.

I'm unapologetic about this now, but I wasn't always; I've spent my whole life taking fire for my fastidiousness, and I've often felt embarrassed about it as a result. My college friends would sneak into my room to move objects on my dresser a couple of inches, then wait to see how long it took me to move them back. I'd catch on right away, of course, and try to casually nudge everything back into place without anyone noticing; the teasing I got, while affectionate, was merciless.

It was only at Eleven Madison Park that I came to recognize my fanatical attention to detail as a superpower. And while it's not my only one, it was definitely the one that got a workout as we were gearing up for our first review.

The restaurant business—any service business, in fact—is a hard one for a perfectionist, because they're human-powered organizations. And, no matter how hard they try, humans make mistakes.

Two responses are possible when you realize that perfection is unattainable: either give up altogether, or try to get as close as you possibly can. At EMP, we opted for the second. **It may not be possible to do *everything* perfectly, but it is possible to do *many things* perfectly.** That's the very definition of excellence: getting as many details right as you can.

Sir David Brailsford was a coach hired to revitalize British cycling. He did so by committing to what he called "the aggregation of marginal gains," or a small improvement in a lot of areas. In his words: "The whole principle came from the idea that if you broke down everything you could think of that goes into riding a bike, and then improve it by 1 percent, you will get a significant increase when you put them all together."

This resonates deeply with me and is a pretty accurate description of how we approached that review season. Perfection as an overall goal was overwhelming, not to mention unattainable—we knew that. But we were going to get as close as we could, and we were on it long before the maître d' told me Frank Bruni was sitting at table 32.

Every restaurant locker room and kitchen in New York City has a picture of *The New York Times* food critic taped to the wall. The role is supposed to be anonymous, but no matter how hard a new critic tries to scrub the internet of photos, an old book jacket or a publicity party picture always squeaks through. (These days it's often a blurry shot, surreptitiously snapped and circulated by another restaurant manager.)

Here's the thing: it doesn't matter if you recognize the critic. No football team phones it in for twenty games, then steps it all the way up for the Super Bowl. Similarly, you can't be a mediocre restaurant three hundred and sixty-four days a year, then transform into a great one the day the critic happens to come in.

Sure, if you recognize the critic before they're seated, you can take them to a table in your most skillful server's section; you can make sure the food you bring them is perfectly plated and the best expression of the dish. But while you can show a critic the best version of your restaurant, you cannot suddenly become something you're not—and they know that, too. The restaurant you are is the restaurant they're reviewing.

Which was why we had spent the months leading up to that moment trying to be a little bit more perfect, every night.

The Littlest Things Matter

We chased excellence in every element of what we did.

The team in the kitchen had trained so they could prepare Daniel's dishes with precision and consistency. Excellent communication between the dining room and the kitchen ensured that the timing was dialed in for every course, at every table.

Everyone working in the dining room had crisply ironed uniforms, tidy hair, and neatly manicured hands. Each piece of silverware and every glass gleamed.

The servers knew the menu backward and forward—where the components for each dish came from and how exactly they were prepared. This is an example of how being unreasonable in the pursuit of excellence made us more hospitable. Because when a server delivered a dish, they didn't have to scramble to remember what was in it; they were so assured in their knowledge, all their energy could go toward connecting with the guest.

Training extended far beyond menu and wine knowledge, to tweaking the most minute aspects of the environment. We couldn't start the evening with the lights too low because our windows were so huge, and the contrast of a too-dim room with the brightness outside was unpleasant. But because the sun goes down at a different time every day (not to mention that the light coming through those massive windows changed dramatically with the weather outside), lowering the light levels over the course of the night wasn't a task we could automate, or make a simple rule about, like "Level 4 at seven p.m."

The staff in charge of adjusting the lights had to be taught, and they had to stay attentive. Maybe more important, they had to understand the impact lighting had on the atmosphere of the room and on the whole experience. They had to buy into the importance of getting it exactly right.

Similarly, we spent hours selecting each song on our music playlists. But music that's too upbeat and loud in a nearly empty room will make you feel like the first guest at the world's most depressing party, so we trained the staff at the front door to gauge when it was time to move from the more mellow Empty Dining Room playlist to the slightly snappier Half-Full Dining Room (and so on), and to control the volume accordingly.

Lighting levels and playlists are details that every restaurant struggles with. But some problems we couldn't solve by being more excellent—we had to innovate.

For instance, it's well-known that at the very beginning of the meal, and at the very end, time seems to slow down. In those moments, the guest has a heightened sensitivity to any delay—we can all relate to feeling like we've been waiting *hours* for that first glass of water or for the check. So it's crucial to get something—anything—in front of the guest as soon as you can.

A glass of water is a great solution, but EMP wasn't a diner on the corner; we couldn't pour water out of a stainless pitcher as soon as a guest was seated. The process we did have in place was too slow. The captain would ask the guest what kind of water they'd like—iced, bottled still, bottled sparkling—then they'd find the table's server to communicate the preference. The server would fetch the bottle and bring it back to the table, a practice made even more glacial because the room was so large.

We spent a lot of time in our manager meetings talking about how to make this more efficient. We ended up stealing a solution from baseball, where the catcher has to communicate with a pitcher sixty feet away: sign language.

After the host brought you to the table, the captain would hand you menus and ask about your water preference. Moments later, and without any visible communication—often before the captain had even left the table—your server would be at the table, pouring your preferred water choice.

It wasn't magic; the captain had discreetly signaled your preference to one of their colleagues using a hand gesture (wiggled fingers for bubbles, a straight chop for still, and a twist of the fist for ice) behind their back.

Another issue was that the room felt *busy*. It took a lot of people to execute hospitality at this level, but too many bodies moving swiftly around a room—even one as big as the dining room at EMP—can feel chaotic. In a bustling brasserie, servers zigzagging through the room lends an exciting energy; in a fine-dining setting, the commotion feels disruptive.

So we established traffic patterns for the staff like the ones on city streets, though they were imperceptible to our guests. Corners had invisible stop or yield signs. Most of the room was one-way only, and the traffic moved clockwise. In a two-way corridor, you hugged the wall to the right, as you would if you were driving.

As we used to say, the goal was ballet, not football. These invisible traffic rules allowed the staff to move in an orderly fashion around the room without dodging one another or relying on verbal cues like "Excuse me" or "Behind."

These subtleties were hidden from the guests, but every single one of them contributed to the overall feeling of comfort and serenity that people enjoyed while they were dining with us.

The Way You Do One Thing Is the Way You Do Everything

We needed to be operating at a high level of precision all the time. To get the staff tuned into the correct frequency, we asked them to start thinking that way as soon as they walked in the door.

We trained the people setting the dining room to place every plate so that if a guest flipped it over to see who had made it, the Limoges stamp would be facing them, right side up.

That's ridiculous, right? Utterly unreasonable. Maybe one or two guests would flip that plate in a month. Most nights, nobody did. Even if they did, would they guess that the placement had been intentional? And some people probably turned over the plate in a way we didn't anticipate, so that the manufacturer's stamp wasn't faceup at all.

That was okay—because whether someone flipped it or not, that perfectly placed plate had already done what it needed to do.

The way you do one thing is the way you do everything, and we found, over and over, that precision in the smallest of details translated to precision in bigger ones. By asking the person setting the dining room to place each plate with total concentration and focus, we were asking them to set the tone for how they'd do everything over the course of the service—how they'd greet our guests, walk through the dining room, communicate with their colleagues, pour the champagne to begin a meal and the cup of coffee to end it.

There's a story about Walt Disney challenging his Imagineers when they were creating the first animatronics for the Enchanted Tiki Room. The Imagineers were convinced they had produced the most lifelike, detailed animatronic bird possible, but Disney wasn't satisfied. Real birds breathed, he pointed out; the chest expanded and contracted. This bird wasn't breathing.

Frustrated, the Imagineers reminded him there would be hundreds of distracting elements in the Tiki Room, including waterfalls, lights, smoke, totem poles, and singing flowers—nobody was going to notice a single bird, whether it was breathing or not. To which Disney responded, "People can feel perfection."

Maybe people don't notice every single individual detail, but in aggregate, they're powerful. In any great business, most of the details you closely attend to are ones that only a tiny, tiny percentage of people will notice. But if I could institute a system that demanded that the entire team think carefully about even the most rudimentary of tasks, I was creating a world in which intention was the standard, and our guests could feel it.

Setting the dining room with intention allowed us to control all the details we *could* control, making us less easily thrown off by everything we couldn't. On any given night, a million problems had the potential to mess up a service. All five of the reservations in our first seating could show up late, guaranteeing that we'd be late to seat the guests arriving for those same tables a few hours later. A guest might walk in irritable from a breakup or from a bad day at work. The espresso machine might stop working.

But there were many things we *could* control. We could ensure that the tablecloths would be spotless and immaculately ironed, the Riedel logo on the foot of each wineglass aligned with the table's edge, and that every piece of silverware had been placed the same distance from the edge of the table—the length of the top joint of the thumb.

We were focusing on those details for the benefit of the guest experience, but the impact they had on us was equally profound; *we* could feel it, too.

Just as walking into a thoughtfully organized room can lower your blood pressure, maybe that perfect tabletop would be enough to remind a flustered server that, no matter how badly in the weeds they felt, the sky was not falling. Maybe seeing that unsullied field of white with glasses and silverware so carefully set by their colleagues would be enough to return them to the frame of mind with which they'd begun the day, allowing them to take a deep breath, recenter themselves, and greet our guests calmly and with warmth: "Welcome to Eleven Madison Park."

Finish Strong: The One-Inch Rule

Say you take a plate from the kitchen and carry it out into the dining room carefully, so that it appears exactly as the chef plated it—the sauce perfect, the tiny pluche of chervil balanced just so. Then, in your rush to your next task, you jostle the plate as you drop it off at the table. Maybe the fish tips over slightly, or the garnish slips.

When you lose focus in that last inch, the presentation is ruined.

A lot of people would say that's not the end of the world, and maybe they're right. But I believe that mistake is bigger than a smudge of sauce where it shouldn't be on an otherwise pristine plate.

Every dish we served at Eleven Madison Park was the result of weeks, if not months, of recipe development and testing. The server who'd described it to the guest had painstakingly learned the description and worked hard to paint a picture for the guest, so the dish sounded irresistible. The cooks who'd made it had brought years of training and experience to the faultless preparation and plating of the protein, and the six other components on the plate represented even more hours of labor and care.

If your job was to place that dish in front of the guest, you were the last link in a long chain of people who had invested many hours of work in that dish. If, in that final inch, a zucchini flower tumbled because of your carelessness, you were letting a lot of people down—including the guest, who'd trusted you with a few hours of their life in the expectation that you would blow their minds.

Unfortunately, it's common for people to lose focus in that last inch, compromising all the work they and their teams have done to get where they are. This isn't specific to restaurants, though there are thousands of restaurant-specific examples I can think of—failing to take a minute to make sure that the final settings on your lighting and music are correct before you open, for instance, or neglecting to walk guests to the door at the end of their meal so you can deliver a personal goodbye.

For the team at EMP, the One-Inch Rule was both a literal instruction—to put the plates down gently—and a metaphorical one, a reminder to stay present and to follow through all the way to that last inch, no matter what you might be doing.

The concept of the One-Inch Rule went viral at EMP. I often heard the team refer to it when they talked in pre-meal about other service experiences they'd had. Most important, I heard them talking about it with one another.

I knew a culture of excellence was taking root when, as people grew and moved up through the ranks, they took on the mission of transmitting that culture to newcomers. And the One-Inch Rule was the lesson I was most likely to overhear a more senior employee passing along to someone who was starting out with us.

Being Right Is Irrelevant

It was a busy Tuesday dinner service when one of our guests ordered the beef with bone marrow and brioche, cooked medium rare. Shortly after his plate was delivered, he summoned the server back to the table. "I ordered this medium rare," he protested, "and this is rare."

I watched as the server corrected him. "Actually, sir, that *is* medium rare, but if you'd prefer it medium, I'd be happy to take it back to the kitchen."

Ugh.

The server *was* technically right, according to the doneness chart in a culinary school textbook. (A true medium rare is, for many people, quite a bit more rare than they're expecting.) And I knew he wasn't trying to be rude.

He was being defensive because he didn't want the guest to think we'd made a mistake. He was part of the team gunning for three stars, and with a not-so-secret eye on a fourth—and you don't get four stars by making mistakes.

His instinct was to get the guest what he wanted, right away—that was the good part. But as far as hospitality goes, it didn't matter. Because pride wasn't what that server was communicating. What he was doing was telling the guest he was wrong: "You, sir, don't know a true medium-rare when you see it." Of course the guest felt shamed and rebuked; he had been, even if that was never the intention.

So here we were again, negotiating the delicate balance between excellence and hospitality.

If you've corrected a guest because you don't want them to think you've made a mistake, you've made a much bigger mistake. If hospitality is about creating genuine connection, and if that connection happens only once the guest has let their guard down, shaming them makes it highly unlikely you'll ever be able to get that connection back again.

In pursuing excellence, we were trying to do as many things right as we possibly could. At the same time, we had to let go of the concept of being right, because it meant going against the very essence of what we were trying to do, which was to make people feel great about eating and drinking in our restaurant.

We needed to make sure we were serving our guests, not our egos; as Danny Meyer says, "Being right is irrelevant." So instead of explaining what a true medium-rare looks like, we needed to say, "Absolutely, sir, I'm sorry," before getting the guest a steak cooked exactly the way he wanted it cooked.

It was then that a new mantra at EMP was born: "**Their perception is our reality.**"

Which means: it doesn't matter whether the steak is rare or medium rare. If the guest's perception is that it's undercooked, the only acceptable response is, "Let me fix it." And true hospitality means going one step further and doing everything you can to make sure the situation doesn't repeat itself—in this case, making an internal guest note in our reservations system that this person "orders steak medium rare, but prefers it cooked medium."

It's important for me to make clear that "Their perception is our reality" did not apply in scenarios where a guest was being abusive or disrespectful. The customer *isn't* always right, and it's unhealthy for everyone if you don't have clear and enforced boundaries for yourself and your staff as to what is unacceptable behavior. The line is bright: abuse should not and cannot be tolerated, period.

Still, this adjustment wasn't easy for everyone on the team. "Sucking it up when I know I'm right feels demeaning," a talented server told me, and I knew what she meant. But the credit we got from our guests for making them happy far outweighed any we lost from making a so-called mistake. It's only demeaning to suck it up if you take it personally. Saying sorry, I reminded the team, doesn't mean you're wrong.

Appreciate the Journey

In January 2007, a photographer from *The New York Times* called the restaurant to schedule a photo shoot for the pictures that would accompany the review of Eleven Madison Park, running later that week.

Daniel and I were excited—and anxious, with good reason. Looking back now, I can see what a huge inflection point that review turned out to be, both in the history of the restaurant and in our careers.

Thankfully, it was good news. Bruni asked: "When did you last look at Eleven Madison Park? If the answer is more than a year ago, look again."

All that focus on excellence had paid off. We'd achieved our first goal: three stars from *The New York Times*.

At our first pre-meal after the review, we poured everyone in the kitchen and dining room a little bit of champagne so we could celebrate what we'd all accomplished and how far we'd come.

And I told them to save up a little bit of the feeling they had that afternoon so they could tap back into it when the going got tough, because we had a long way to go. "Have a great service. When you get off, go out and have an awesome time—you deserve it. Feel it all fully. Appreciate this moment. Then come back tomorrow and we'll get back to work."

(When, true to his word, Danny sent Richard Coraine to ask me if I still wanted to move from EMP to Shake Shack, I told him I thought I'd stick around for a while.)

CHAPTER 12

RELATIONSHIPS ARE SIMPLE.
SIMPLE IS HARD.

I LOVE ANY EXCUSE TO wear a tuxedo.

So it was a thrill to put one on and walk down the red carpet at the James Beard Awards in May 2007 at Lincoln Center with chefs like Thomas Keller and Daniel Boulud.

We were there because Daniel had been nominated for the Rising Star Chef of the Year Award, which is given only to chefs under the age of thirty. He had just turned twenty-nine, and though he had been nominated for that award before, while he was chef at Campton Place, he hadn't won. This was his last chance, and I was convinced he was going to take it home.

Then they opened the envelope: "And the 2007 award for Rising Star Chef goes to Momofuku's David Chang!"

Daniel was devastated. And while his name would have been the one on the award, we all felt like we'd lost. Chang's restaurants, you could argue, were a reaction to fine-dining restaurants; he believed you could have delicious food without pretention and stuffiness. But so did we! Daniel and I had been doing everything in our power to prove that fine dining was still relevant and that these hallowed traditions could be reimagined in a way that felt contemporary and fun. The difference was that Chang's restaurants were a rebuke to fine-dining restaurants, whereas we hoped ours represented their evolution.

After the *Times* review, we had started to feel our project might not be such a fool's errand. But on that night, Chang had won, and we'd lost.

It was a tough hit. So immediately after the awards were announced, I started inviting friends to come back to the restaurant with us. Even though I also felt the loss acutely, my responsibility that night was to take care of Daniel. It's easy to be someone's partner during the good times, but it's most important during the hard ones, and I wanted him to feel as loved and supported as he would have if he had won.

Later, we'd be known for the legendary, restaurant-destroying parties we threw when we were celebrating a win. But the first party we ever threw for ourselves was on a day that we lost. It reminded me of our wise guest's advice: drink your best bottle not on your best day but on your worst.

I have never been the kind of leader who brushes off bad feelings. After a setback, I'd tell the team to go ahead and wallow. "Guys, this sucks. We're working so hard, and we care so much, and still—today didn't go our way. Let's allow ourselves to feel the disappointment; it's real and we don't need to pretend it's not."

Fully feel your disappointment, sure—but there's no reason you should drink bad wine while you're doing it. So the night of the Beard Awards, Richard Coraine went to our cellar and emerged with some beautiful bottles. We filled the room with people who loved us and believed in us. Daniel Boulud came downtown and made scrambled eggs for everyone, as he had when I was in college. (I had a slightly better kitchen to offer him this time.)

The party wasn't an all-out rager, but it was a celebration: No James Beard committee could take away how much of himself Daniel had put into the pursuit of his goal or how much he'd accomplished. And even though we'd lost, the award ceremony itself had felt like an arrival of sorts. It had been electrifying to realize we were suddenly on the radar screens of people whose work we had followed our whole careers.

That night was a hard one. But it wasn't devastating because making the choice to be together—to lift one another up—brought us even closer together.

Turn Toward Tension

Working in a restaurant is challenging: a lot needs to be done, and quickly. There are stairs to climb, hot kitchens, and guests with competing desires and requests. People on the team from all walks of life have to learn to navigate relationships with one another.

While we'd gotten to the point where everyone who worked at EMP was pushing for the same result—every single one of us wanted to make the restaurant the best it could be—we didn't always agree on the best way to achieve it.

And whatever friction those differing opinions might have caused between us was exacerbated by how badly we all wanted to succeed. I've seen this in other companies, where everyone cares so much about the mission, they forget to care about one another. Our collective passion—one of our greatest strengths—was in danger of becoming a dangerous weakness.

Given everything we'd done to build a culture of collaboration, excellence, and leadership, we needed to learn how to embrace tension, too, or everything we'd built would be lost.

Don't Go to Bed Angry

We started with that old chestnut people tell honeymooners: Don't go to bed angry. (Now that I'm married, I'm not certain this is the best marital advice, but I stand by it as far as professional relationships are concerned.)

We went so far as to make this a rule, drilled over and over in pre-meal: don't leave work if you're harboring feelings of frustration or resentment toward a colleague or the job itself; make sure to talk things through before heading home.

In the heat of service, a seemingly minor disagreement—for example, whether it's more important to get a check down on table 28 before clearing dessert plates from 24—could easily mushroom into a situation where two excellent people weren't communicating at all. But because we'd talked about this so much in pre-meal, all a manager would have to say to them at the end of the night were those five words: "Don't go to bed angry."

Thirty minutes later, you'd see the two servers talking in the hallway—and the next night, they'd have a fantastic service together in the same section.

In my experience, people usually want to be heard more than they want to be agreed with. Even if neither of them managed to change the other's mind, at the very least they'd have shown each other respect by taking the time to listen. Even if they didn't achieve resolution, they'd both feel lighter when they headed off to bed.

Find the Third Option

I remember a battle Daniel and I had after our first big renovation.

A charger is the decorative plate waiting at your place setting when you arrive at many fine-dining restaurants. You don't eat off these plates; in fact, they're generally removed before the first course arrives.

I think they're dumb.

To me, the presence of a charger on the table is a textbook example of one of those unexamined fine-dining rules: if they exist only for show, add absolutely nothing to the guest's experience, and are taken away immediately, what's the point?

But Daniel, with his classic European background, was adamant that even a beautifully set table looked undressed without them.

We went round and round like this for hours: I thought they were useless; he thought they were beautiful.

To break a stalemate, we would sometimes try swapping sides. It's easy for passionate people to get entrenched in their respective positions. But you can't help but connect with a position when you're arguing for it, and swapping sides tends to jog you out of a stubborn focus on "your" idea. You can stop worrying about winning and can start thinking about what's right for the organization.

Unfortunately, in this case, it didn't work.

I don't remember now who introduced the third option, but eventually one was put on the table—literally and figuratively: What if we kept the charger but made it useful?

We called our brilliant ceramics designer Jono Pandolfi—a friend of mine from high school—who worked with us to design chargers with a beautiful unglazed circle in the middle. That circle was precisely sized for the foot of the bowl of the amuse-bouche, the single-bite gift from the kitchen that opens a fine-dining meal.

Out of the engagement, the two of us had stumbled upon a more graceful and hospitable solution, one neither of us would ever have come up with on our own.

To me, the symbolism was beautiful. If you were experienced with fine dining, you sat down expecting those chargers to be whisked away. Instead, they stayed on the table, ready to offer our guests a gift. Daniel got tables dressed with beautiful, custom-made ceramics, and I could rest easy knowing the charger wasn't superfluous, an empty nod to form, but graciously poised to receive the guest's first course.

Concede the Win

For the winter menu one year, Daniel wanted to do three separate dessert courses after the cheese. I was worried about dragging out the meal and losing people's attention. The whey sorbet was utterly delicious, but does anyone really rave about a sorbet course? Couldn't we—shouldn't we— keep it moving?

Daniel was adamant. He'd put a lot of work into each one of those dessert courses and had thought seriously about the guest's experience of the meal. Eventually, after a lot of back and forth, he said, "It's important to me." That was all he needed to say. I went back to the dining room team and told them we'd have to control the pace on our end by increasing how efficiently we served and bussed those courses.

Sometimes, the only way to proceed in pursuit of a good partnership is to decide that whoever cares more about the issue can have their way. It wasn't that I didn't care about how many desserts we served—when you're intense and detail-oriented, everything matters. But it was *more* important to Daniel than it was to me.

There was an unwritten corollary to this rule, which is that neither of us could abuse the "It's important to me" card by pulling it too many times. Mostly, though, we found that the willingness of the other person to relinquish their own position helped to build trust between us.

Sometimes, though, we had to duke it out.

Learn Their Tough-Love Language

One of my close friends is an even-tempered, laid-back guy, beloved by the people who work for him. Over dinner one night, he mentioned he was getting frustrated with one of his employees, who had a nasty habit of undermining new managers by talking smack about them with less senior staff.

"I keep telling him that he can't continue doing this," my friend complained, exasperated. "But I found out Friday that he's gone and done it again. I don't seem to be getting through to him."

"Have you tried yelling at him?" I asked.

I've spent my career crusading against toxic workplace cultures. Certainly, if the last ten years has taught us anything, especially in the restaurant industry, it's that company cultures based on abuse and harassment and manipulation are not only awful and unethical, but unstable and inefficient as well.

And yet that doesn't—in fact, it cannot—mean your culture should be 100 percent sweetness and light.

Managing staff boils down to two things: how you praise people, and how you criticize them. Praise, I might argue, is the more important of the two. **But you cannot establish any standard of excellence without criticism, so a thoughtful approach to how you correct people must be a part of your culture, too.**

One of Richard Coraine's most often repeated sayings was "One size fits one." He was referring to the hospitality experience: some guests love it when you hang out at the table and schmooze, while others want you to take their order and disappear. It's your job to read the guest and to serve them how they want to be served.

Similarly, there's no one-size-fits-all rule for managing people.

Gary Chapman saved a lot of romantic relationships with his 1992 book, *The Five Love Languages*, which delineates the five general ways people show and prefer to experience love. (They are: acts of service, gift-giving, physical touch, quality time, and words of affirmation.)

Chapman noted that people tend to go wrong by showing love the way they want to receive it. If your partner's love language is acts of service, for instance, bringing them a cup of coffee prepared exactly how they like it is going to land better than surprising them with a kiss—even if that's what *you'd* most like.

Just as certain expressions of love work better for some people than others, so do different expressions of tough love. I'm not sure there are five tough-love languages, but there are people for whom a polite correction will not land; those people need a little fire.

I knew when we started to work together that Daniel's managerial style was different from mine. Of course it was! I'd come up in the lovey-dovey, uber-respectful world of Danny Meyer's Enlightened Hospitality. Daniel, on the other hand, had been working since the age of fourteen in the aggressive, militant kitchens of Europe's three-star Michelin restaurants, where screaming and humiliation—and often worse—were standard workplace conditions.

He'd always been on his best behavior when I was with him, but stories circulated among the staff about his temper, and I'd talked to him a number of times about what I'd heard. "C'mon, man," I'd say. "You don't want to be one of those lunatic chefs." He'd laugh and agree with me—then, a week later, I'd hear another story about him losing it on someone.

One day, I happened to be in the kitchen when a cook put up an incorrectly plated crab roulade with avocado. Daniel picked the food up with his hands and threw it right back into the cook's face.

My mouth fell open; I could not *believe* what I had just seen.

It was absolutely unacceptable.

I dragged him down the hallway into our office, and, for the first time in my professional career, I screamed at someone I worked with.

"If you're going to throw food into people's faces, I want nothing to do with you. You're incredible, and I love what we're doing here, but you need to decide right now what kind of leader you want to be. Because if that's how your kitchen is going to operate, then you're doing this without me. You can find somebody else to run this restaurant with."

I'm good at apologizing when, in the heat of a Friday-night service, my tone betrays any frustration I might be feeling, and there are people who have worked for me for fifteen years who have never heard me yell— but some have. And in this case, the only way I was going to get through to Daniel was with a confrontation this extreme, complete with raised voice and an ultimatum I was prepared to follow through on.

He never threw a roulade or anything else again. In fact, he tells this story himself in the limited-edition version of our book *Eleven Madison Park: The Next Chapter*, citing that incident and my response to it as a turning point.

You have to know the people you're working with. Some people are totally pragmatic about criticism; correct them privately and without emotion, and they'll receive the reproach in exactly the spirit in which it's offered. Three minutes later, they'll have apologized for the mistake, taken the note, and the two of you will have moved on to chatting about last night's Mets game.

Other folks are sensitive to criticism. This isn't necessarily a negative characteristic—it's usually an indication they want to do a good job and feel deeply wounded at any suggestion that they haven't. But those people are going to react, no matter what you say or how gently and diplomatically you say it, so you'd better spend some time planning exactly how you're going to deliver the feedback. And you'd be wise to budget time to spend with them afterward, so you can sit with them and let them know that they're still loved.

Then there are the people who can't or won't hear what you're saying unless it comes with a little thunder. If your reprimand is too mild and conversational, they won't believe you're serious. With these people, you're going to have to get into it a little bit, even if that's not your usual managerial style.

My even-tempered friend reported that it had been uncomfortable for him to raise his voice with the problem employee. But he had, and I was pleased and not surprised to hear that when he did, he'd finally made real headway with the guy.

It's important to note that even this kind of reproach needs to be delivered, per Ken Blanchard, privately and without emotion. When I dragged Daniel into the office, my voice may have been loud, but my words were measured; I was emotional about the situation, but that didn't come through in my delivery. You're still criticizing the behavior, not the person, and a raised voice doesn't mean losing control and raging. (In fact, you absolutely *cannot* lose control and rage.) It's simply a different tough-love language, one that's louder and sterner than the one you naturally prefer.

I should mention here there's one tough-love language that will never, ever work, and that's sarcasm. Managers, especially young ones, will sometimes try to shroud criticism in humor because they're insecure about delivering a rebuke. But **sarcasm is *always* the wrong medium for a serious communication**. It demeans the person who's receiving the criticism, the message you're delivering, and, frankly, you as well.

Most of us have no difficulty at all in delivering praise; that's the fun part of being a boss. But it's hard to criticize someone. So I spend a lot of time with my managers talking about criticism—how to deliver it, how to receive it, and maybe most important, how to think about it. We all want to be liked, and when you give someone a note about what they could be doing differently and better, you run the risk of losing their goodwill. That's why I say there is no better way to show someone you care than by being willing to offer them a correction; it's the purest expression of putting someone else's needs above your own, which is what hospitality is all about. **Praise is affirmation, but criticism is *investment*.**

And this is why it's so important, no matter where you are in the hierarchy, to be able to graciously receive criticism, too. It's natural to bristle a little when you come up short, particularly if you're an A student who takes pride in your work. But if your response is consistently defensive, if you always push back or insist on justifying your mistakes, people are eventually going to stop coming to you with notes. You've made it too unpleasant for them to continue, and they're going to stop investing in you—and you're going to stop growing as a result.

Hire Slow, Fire Fast—But Not Too Fast

One night, a manager reported that he'd caught one of our best captains—I'll call him Ben—drinking during service. If a restaurant doesn't allow drinking on the job (and we did not; some do), this is grounds for immediate dismissal. But instead of immediately telling him to pack his bags, I asked him to sit down and talk to me.

"I'm going to ask you not to lie to me: Were you drinking last night during your shift?"

He hung his head. "Yes. I'm sorry, and I completely understand if you fire me over it."

I said, "I'm not firing you yet, but I'm not happy. You didn't let me down—or, rather, you didn't *just* let me down; you disappointed your entire team. You're supposed to be a leader, but instead of leading, you got drunk.

"So we can do this one of two ways. You can leave right now—we'll shake hands, I'll thank you for all the time you've given us and all the people you've made happy, and how much you've done to make this restaurant a better place. Then you can clean out your locker and go home.

"But if you want to stay, then take tomorrow off, come back the day after, and apologize to everybody you were working with last night. Tell them what you did, why you realize it's a mistake, and why you're sorry. Promise you'll never do it again—and know that if you do, I'm going to fire you on the spot."

It wasn't easy for Ben to have those conversations with his colleagues.

He was a tough captain to work for because his standards were high; if you were in his station, he held you accountable. But there is tremendous power in vulnerability. Because Ben took responsibility, everyone who'd been furious with him forgave him.

A couple of months later, Ben drank again during a shift, and I fired him, as I'd said I would. (I'm happy to report it served as a wake-up call; he's in recovery now and has made a notable career for himself in hospitality.) But I have no regrets about giving him a second chance.

The people you work with will never be your actual family. That doesn't mean that you can't work harder to treat them like family, which may mean tweaking one of the great management sayings out there, which is "Hire slow and fire fast."

I do believe, as I've already said, in hiring slow. You need to be acutely aware in the first few months if someone joining the team is not the right fit, or if they're simply going to need a little extra support to succeed. And you can't drag your feet unnecessarily on firing someone who's toxic; you need to get them out before they poison the balance of the team.

At the same time, you would never kick a member of your family out of the house for making a single mistake, would you? So maybe we should amend that saying to "Hire slow, fire fast—but not *too* fast."

Create Your Own Traditions

In 2007, we opened for Thanksgiving for the first time.

Danny's restaurants had never opened for any of the major holidays: Thanksgiving, Christmas Eve, Christmas Day, or New Year's Day. It was a gift from him to his employees, a financial sacrifice so the people who worked for him could spend time with their loved ones.

But I wanted to serve Thanksgiving at Eleven Madison Park.

I talked to Paul Bolles-Beaven, one of Danny's partners, before I approached Danny. "He's never going to go for it," he told me. "This is an important, well-established part of the company culture."

But Danny is always open to being challenged, and if you come to him with a measured, thoughtful argument, he'll listen to what you have to say. So I made my case. On the one hand, yes: it's lovely to have Thanksgiving Day off to rest and celebrate with your family. But most people who work in New York City restaurants aren't *from* New York City, so most of them weren't able to use that day off to go home to celebrate anyway.

On the other hand, with the money we'd make from staying open and serving all day, we'd be able to afford to close the restaurant the first few days of January, giving people enough time to go home. We were still giving the staff a gift—but one they could really use.

Danny agreed.

Danny's willingness to reevaluate that holiday policy was a reminder to me that **no aspect of your business should be off-limits to reevaluation**. I told the staff this story whenever I was encouraging them to come forward with ideas. "Don't be shy. Even if we're proud of the way we do something—even if it feels integral to the restaurant—that doesn't mean we couldn't be doing it better: more elegantly, more efficiently, more creatively. Nothing is sacred."

That first year, Thanksgiving reservations sold out as soon as they were released. It helped that there weren't that many great restaurants open for the holiday in New York. It has gone on to be one of the busiest days of the year for us, every year.

It was also one of the best days to work, to the point where the team fought over that shift. I loved it and worked it myself every year; it wasn't until after I was married that I'd leave before the very end.

Daniel had little experience with this most American of holidays, so we worked with his sous-chefs to develop the menu. We'd hold one long service over the course of the day. And once we were finished serving the last guests, the entire staff would sit down for our own Thanksgiving dinner.

For the team, it would be a real Thanksgiving, as I grew up celebrating it, with delicious food, family gathered around a table, and words of thanks. We'd push the tables together to make a huge one in the center of that glorious dining room, load our plates, open some wine, and go around the entire table so everyone could share what they were thankful for.

Food for the staff was factored into the kitchen's preparations for the day. Our dinner wouldn't be an afterthought, reheated food that hadn't made it onto other people's plates. Instead, we'd enjoy exactly the same meal we'd spent the day giving to others, served buffet-style. Meanwhile, our wine director, John Ragan, had saved lots of unsolicited bottles that wine reps had dropped off to be sampled, so there would be plenty of good things to drink.

Every Labor Day, Floyd Cardoz and his brilliant wife, Barkha, threw a barbecue at their house in New Jersey for the employees at Tabla. There, Floyd would trade his crisp chef whites for a decidedly uncool suburban-dad outfit while he was manning the grill, but seeing him that way only made us respect him more. He showed me by example that I could be myself without losing any of my credibility as an authority figure and a boss—and that I should.

That first Thanksgiving, and every one after, I gave the first toast.

I spoke from the heart. I told them I was grateful to finally be in a place where I didn't need to hide my neuroses, or to be embarrassed about them. That got a laugh, not only because everyone there had been on the receiving end of my perfectionism, but also because everyone around that table had spent some portion of their working lives pretending they didn't care as much as they did, for fear of being mocked. At EMP, we all felt like we belonged. Every day, our colleagues challenged *us* to be better, instead of always—always—the other way around.

Then we went around the table, and everyone took a turn. It didn't hurt that the wine was flowing; even those who ordinarily played their cards close to their chest started sharing. It was incredible to watch people seize the opportunity to be open and emotional with their peers.

People who are gifted at hospitality tend to be sensitive. They notice everything, feel deeply, and care a lot. These are superpowers, though that tenderness can also make them a handful to manage. I've heard many frustrated managers complain about these employees: "They're so needy! They need so much reinforcement! I have to walk them through every decision; I have to hold their hands through every change!"

But these tendencies are often what make these people so good at their work; they need to have delicate antennae. It takes compassion to know when a guest is intimidated by the room—and a light touch to dial back the formality so they don't feel condescended to. If a server's Spidey sense tells them a table is getting frustrated by how long the food is taking, they can check on the entrée and apologize before the guest has even complained. And a server who is preternaturally alert to other people will realize there's tension at a table as soon as they approach; they can then pace the courses so the guests can resolve the issue between them before moving on to enjoying the rest of their meal.

I knew these sensitive people needed extra time and love. But those Thanksgiving toasts created a space where the staff could be vulnerable with their peers, and they needed that, too. **If you don't create room for the people who work for you to feel seen and heard in a team setting, they'll never be fully known by the people around them.**

Establishing your own traditions, as we did with Thanksgiving, is part of a layered and nuanced culture. One of my dad's quotes I love the most is: "The secret to happiness is always having something to look forward to." This was one of the reasons, aside from the fear and grief, that people had such a hard time during the COVID lockdowns. With no theater or sports events or even a date-night dinner to look forward to, it was hard to keep your spirits up.

It's true within organizations, too, especially when you're hustling. We'd pushed hard for three stars, but it was nothing in comparison to how we'd push later. Every year, we *needed* something to look forward to, and Thanksgiving became one of the beautiful traditions we could count on.

These new-fashioned traditions are essential to a healthy culture, but—ugh, birthday cake in the break room—they tend not to stick unless people enjoy and look forward to them. **New traditions work only if they're authentic—if they fill a real purpose and satisfy a real need.** This was definitely key to our Thanksgiving success, as restaurant workers on major holidays tend to feel a little like the Lost Boys from *Peter Pan*—hungry and unloved.

The meals restaurant staff share together before service is called family meal, though it usually feels more like a bunch of colleagues hurriedly shoving calories into themselves before setting the dining room. That Thanksgiving, for the first time, we *did* feel like a family sitting down together to eat.

CHAPTER 13

LEVERAGING AFFIRMATION

Founded in 1954, Relais & Châteaux is an association of some of the best independent restaurants and hotels in the world.

You pay to be a part of it, but you have to be accepted, and the guidelines are notoriously stringent. Most Relais properties are historic landmarks, and the restaurants they include are excellent. To give you an idea of the company we were hoping to keep: when we applied, the American restaurants on the list included the French Laundry, Daniel, Le Bernardin, the Inn at Little Washington, Jean-Georges, and Per Se.

Michelin stars and *New York Times* reviews aren't honors you can ask for; you work hard, try to be the best you can be, and hope they show up to evaluate you. But you apply to Relais when you think you're ready, and in 2008, Daniel and I thought we were.

The three-star *New York Times* review we'd gotten had been great for business and for our morale. And while we weren't shy about the fact that we were gunning for four stars, it's usually at least five years between reviews. In order to maintain our momentum, we wanted another respected, external entity to say, "This is one of the great restaurants in America," and there weren't many outlets that could do that.

But when we asked Danny if we could apply, he said no. "Sorry, guys,

ings magazine is not a major media splash. But it was the first time my name had been mentioned in the press, and I was really proud. I went to the newsstand and bought multiple copies, including one to send to my dad.

As EMP started getting more and more press, I made sure to turn the spotlight on those who deserved it, making them the stars of the show. If a PR person reached out about our beer program, I put them in touch with Kirk Kelewae, the guy who ran it, and made sure it was Kirk's name that appeared in the subsequent article.

Not only did this ensure Kirk was getting the credit he so richly deserved, but it got everyone else on the team thinking, *Wait a minute! I want that kind of recognition, too.*

Unfortunately, the opposite problem happens so often, it needs to be addressed directly: **Don't take credit for other people's work.**

I can't count the number of times I've opened *Bon Appétit* or *Food & Wine* to see a chef offering a recipe one of their talented sous-chefs came up with, or an owner bragging about developing a beverage program that has their sommelier's fingerprints all over it.

One particularly brazen example: I was scrolling through Instagram one afternoon and stumbled on a post by a famous chef—a photo of his "inspiration" for one of his restaurant's most gorgeous signature dishes. Nobody was surprised when, a short while later, the brilliant sous-chef who'd actually come up with every aspect of the dish—including its trademark presentation—left for an opportunity at another restaurant.

I get plenty of media attention, and I don't need the world to think I'm a genius about beer when I basically couldn't have told you the difference between a pilsner and a Dr Pepper before Kirk got ahold of me. In fact, as a leader, I'd rather get attention for creating the conditions that enabled Kirk to put together an award-winning beer program.

Friends in management positions at other restaurants thought my strategy was misguided. "They're gonna get poached," they warned me every time someone on my staff got a complimentary write-up.

They were right, in a way; the more attention people got, the more job offers they got, too. But I prefer to make decisions based on hope, rather than fear. The onus was on me to take such great care of my people they wouldn't want to leave. In general, it worked—probably because it was clear we were gearing up for greatness, and the talented people we'd hired could smell that in the air.

Sometimes people we directed attention toward did end up leaving us. My philosophy was: so be it. People are going to move on, and I'd rather they leave feeling like heroes. Alums of our restaurant, out there doing extraordinary work? That was good for us, too.

It was worth the risk, because the more mini-celebrities I had on staff, the longer the line of people outside was, banging on the door to work with us. And it relieved the pressure on me and Daniel, too, because with every article, the likelihood increased that a guest who came to the restaurant would have contact with a staff member they'd heard of or read about.

It's not lost on me that not all businesses have the relationship with the media that restaurants do. But every business has external stakeholders, whether those are board members, social media followers, or members of the community you belong to. When someone out there catches your company doing something right, leverage it, and **when that external affirmation comes, direct it to the people responsible**.

If a distributor compliments you on always getting your orders in on time, ask them to say it again once you've gotten the person responsible on the phone. If an investor notes that the reports you send are always timely and detailed and clear, grab the accountant who puts those reports together and pull them into the meeting so they can bask in the praise.

Use Every Tool in Your Tool Kit

When a server or one of the managers pulled off an amazing act of hospitality, I made sure the higher-ups at Union Square Hospitality Group knew all about it.

Yes, it was a means to stay in touch, to let them know we had it on lock; I didn't mind reporting that my team was killing it. But forwarding an email we'd gotten from a thrilled customer wasn't about making myself look good; it was a way to arm Danny with information he could use the next time he stopped by.

If I'd forwarded a rave from a guest about the charming and attentive service they'd received, Danny could pull aside the responsible captain to say thanks. If he knew a reservationist had gone above and beyond to secure a table for a special anniversary, he could compliment her directly on the job she'd done.

As a leader, you have to use every single tool in your kit to build morale and keep it high. This is a constant quest for a manager, a daily pursuit—and it's hard to do. I like to think my team respected me and were inspired by me, and that a word of affirmation from me went a long way. But the reality was that we spent all day every day together, and no compliment I could give would have the impact of one from someone in a more senior position. Especially when the head of the company was Danny Meyer, whom everybody loved and respected so much.

It's common for a leader to want the people on their team to see them as the ultimate authority figure and to box out their bosses as a result. That's a lack of confidence, and it's shortsighted. Randy Garutti, my old boss from Tabla, never worried I had less respect for him because Danny Meyer praised me; if anything, he could see I worked harder as a result of it.

I knew better than anyone that a word of thanks from Danny was rocket fuel. Rather than feel insecure about that, why not use it to our collective advantage? So I kept forwarding those emails, making sure to gather a plentiful supply of that fuel for the people who worked for me.

Persistence and Determination Alone Are Omnipotent

Hosting Daniel Boulud, Thomas Keller, and Patrick O'Connell had everyone walking a little taller. Being unreasonable was working, and the team could feel it.

Those three chefs could feel it, too. All three sent letters to Relais & Châteaux, saying we were one of the great restaurants in New York, and it would be a mistake to wait another year before evaluating us.

(Ironically, with three of the most renowned chefs in America writing us personal recommendation letters, we had a stronger application as latecomers than we would have had if we'd made the deadline in the first place.)

Relais sent an anonymous reviewer; we had no idea who they were or when they visited. Apparently, though, they had a good time, because we found out a few months later we'd been accepted to the association.

It was a tremendous honor to hang that plaque outside the restaurant—and deeply meaningful for Daniel, who had come up in Europe, where the award is even more esteemed. It was also the first time any organization of significance had put us on the same level as restaurants like Daniel and Le Bernardin and Jean-Georges and Per Se.

Another plaque had come into my life, earlier. When I was little, my dad gave me one engraved with his favorite quote, from Calvin Coolidge.

I had it hanging in my childhood bedroom, then in my college dorm room; I have it still, hanging here above my desk.

It reads:

> *Nothing in this world can take the place of*
> *persistence. Talent will not; nothing is more*
> *common than unsuccessful men with talent.*
> *Genius will not; unrewarded genius is almost*
> *a proverb. Education will not; the world is*
> *full of educated derelicts. Persistence and*
> *determination alone are omnipotent.*

It would have been easy to give up on Relais & Châteaux after Danny said we weren't ready. And yes, it would have been absolutely mortifying if we'd gotten rejected after I'd pushed him to let us apply. But you don't reach the top by taking no for an answer, especially not the first time you get it. We needed to be willing to fail.

Our acceptance into Relais & Châteaux added immeasurably to our momentum; their affirmation encouraged a lot of people to give us a fresh look. We leveraged that accolade, and it helped take us further down the road. And seeing the effect those three chefs in our dining room had on the team showed me how valuable affirmation could be for our culture, if we leveraged it. Sure, receiving praise feels good, but the dopamine hit lasts only so long. Being intentional in using that praise to encourage, inspire, and uplift our team could shift us into a whole new gear.

CHAPTER 14

RESTORING BALANCE

AMBITION IS AN EXTRAORDINARY THING, a nuclear reactor that provides unlimited amounts of energy. Getting accepted into Relais & Châteaux gave us a taste of success, and we wanted more . . . a lot more.

It was 2008. I was twenty-eight years old. I wasn't married; I didn't have any kids yet. Eleven Madison Park was *everything* to me.

I wasn't alone; the entire leadership team was consumed by ambition. We were working all the time, driven by the force of all the unreasonable goals we'd set for ourselves and for the restaurant.

We wanted EMP to be a four-star restaurant, not a very good three-star restaurant.

And because of how badly we wanted to achieve that goal and the passion we were bringing to our pursuit of it every single day, the team was right there with us, throwing all of themselves into the work, too. The entire dining room team was so polished, so eager, it became almost a game to see what tiny service detail we could improve by making it more complicated. In the kitchen, Daniel and his team were adding ever more intricate components to the dishes. Prep lists were getting longer, techniques more complex. We were all doing whatever it took to push the experience to the next level.

We were on fire.

Then, one night at eleven p.m., a cook who worked the morning shift ran through the doors in a panic. In her sleeplessness and stress and disorientation, she thought she was two hours late for her nine a.m. shift; in reality, she was ten hours early.

There had probably been other indications we were going too fast, but that one made us pull up and say whoa. In that moment it became clear: our ambition had gotten the better of us. The nuclear reactor was melting down.

Much is written about how leaders need to have the vision to look ahead; in my opinion, not enough is written about how leaders also need to have the awareness to look down, to see what's really beneath their feet. Like Wile E. Coyote, we'd been so focused on catching the Road Runner, we'd run right off the cliff without realizing it. We'd been so focused on managing the guest experience, we'd forgotten to manage our culture.

We'd lost our balance, and we needed to get it back.

Slow Down to Speed Up

Kevin Boehm, the CEO and cofounder of Chicago's Boka restaurant group, spoke movingly at the Welcome Conference about a difficult period he'd gone through at precisely the moment when everything in his life seemed to be going beautifully.

He told a captivated room how he'd spent his whole life raising his hand to say yes and how he'd mistakenly come to believe this was why he was depressed and anxious. What he came to realize, though, was this:

> I can only be authentic and inspirational and
> restorative if I buy back the time to restore
> myself. . . . This is not a passive pursuit;
> it's active. The things I can control—

mindfulness, diet, exercise, attitude, and
whom I choose to spend my time with—those
things take priority over all others. So when I
do raise my hand, I'm armed with the mental
fortitude to make sure that my ambition
doesn't undermine the clarity that got me all
these killer opportunities in the first place.

When I heard this, I felt a shock of recognition. The safety instructions the flight attendant delivers before takeoff are clear: "Put your own
oxygen mask on first before assisting others." But when you're in the
hospitality industry, that instruction can feel counterintuitive. Aren't we
supposed to put others first and attend to them before we attend to ourselves?

The answer is no. If you aren't tending to your own needs, you can't
help those around you. Pride and ambition motivated us to push—to
tweak, to optimize, to work harder, demanding more of ourselves and
those around us each day. But you can't pour endlessly from your own
pitcher without ever stopping to refill it.

So, with some deliberation—and even a little sadness—Daniel and I
decided we needed to slow down.

We stopped changing the menu as frequently, so everyone had more
time to catch up. We hired more people, so the existing staff wouldn't
be spread too thin. We cut many of the flourishes we'd added to service.
To give one small example, we'd been pouring many of the sauces and
adding additional components to the dishes tableside. Because we had to
bring those to the table on a separate tray, we needed twice as many food
runners. But we didn't have twice as many food runners, so more often
than not, it was a dining room manager following with that tray. To al-
leviate some pressure, we went back to saucing the dishes in the kitchen.
Though marginally less theatrical, the change meant the managers could
return to supporting the team on the floor.

It was a shame to lose those extras; many of our guests noticed their absence. But keeping them wasn't worth the cost, if doing too much meant the staff was falling apart. I reminded myself: If adding another element to the experience means you're going to do everything a little less well, walk it back. **Do less, and do it well.**

The cultural reboot was probably most apparent in the topics we tackled at pre-meal. For months, the focus had been on how we could excel and achieve. Now, it was time to bring that same creativity and innovation to setting up the staff to succeed in a more sustainable way.

Everyone's oxygen is different, and we have to figure out for ourselves what we need to breathe. For me, relaxation means a night alone on the couch, eating Chinese takeout while binge-watching television too dumb to disclose. My wife's oxygen is a hike or a long run.

Yours might be CrossFit, or yoga, or a long bike ride, or cooking, or painting, or going to see live music, or lying on a blanket in the park with your friends. Exercise, nature, being in community, and creative pursuits do seem to be common themes, but it's never going to be one-size-fits-all: you have to know what works for you.

This was what we worked on with the team. We encouraged them to find their oxygen and to take the time to breathe. Slowing down wasn't just about nurturing them in the moment. It was about building a more solid foundation for the future, so that when we did need to speed up again (and we would, very soon), our minds and hearts were in top shape.

The Deep Breathing Club

My good friend Andrew Tepper worked for years in a juvenile psychiatric hospital. When he started there, he was alarmed to see how many kids were regularly melting down or freaking out, threatening to hurt themselves and others. He was also disturbed by how many sedatives the staff was prescribing.

He started teaching the kids calming breathing techniques to use when they were agitated. Though the techniques were incredibly effective, he struggled to get the kids to do them consistently. (A good idea is one thing; getting it to take root is another.) Then, one day a few months later, while rummaging through his parents' basement, he happened upon some silk screen equipment he'd held on to from high school.

He used the silk screens to make a batch of really cool T-shirts with the letters DBC (Deep Breathing Club) in block letters across the front. If a kid got through three potential incidents by using deep breathing instead of screaming or getting violent, they'd earn a shirt. He was simultaneously reinforcing good behavior and making deep breathing cool.

Fast-forward five months, and half the kids in the hospital were wearing DBC shirts. The number of meltdowns, as well as the amount of sedatives prescribed, went down significantly.

We were having our own version of a collective meltdown at EMP. Oxygen masks were one thing—a necessary big-picture solution. But we also needed a solution *in the moment.*

You know when you're in the weeds, all the way at your wits' end, and you're so overwhelmed you can't even tell what would help? Crisis moments like that happen often in restaurants and in most high-pressure environments. If you have any emotional intelligence at all, you know that saying "Calm down" or "Chill out" to a person who is freaking out is like squirting lighter fluid on a bonfire already on the verge of spreading out of control.

But still: there has to be a phrase, a rescue remedy that will bring the other person back to themselves long enough to ask for the help they need. Because much of the time, a simple intervention—like asking a manager to bring a table the silverware for their next course—is all it would take to give the panicked person some breathing room.

I invited Andrew to pre-meal to tell the team about DBC, the idea that a few deep breaths can be all it takes to get you through what feels like an impossible situation. (He brought T-shirts.) The concept became one of the most enduring elements of our culture. In moments of crisis, all we had to do was walk up to an overwhelmed colleague and say, "DBC." They'd stop and take a few deep breaths. What was really being communicated was, "I see you and what you're going through. We're in this together, and we're going to get through it together, so what can I do *right now* to help?"

Touch the Lapel

Our manager meetings became less about improving the guest experience and more about how to make the restaurant more sustainable for all of us. Our pre-meal meetings followed suit, almost exclusively consumed with conversations about how to restore balance.

Because the culture of collaboration was fully in place at Eleven Madison Park, it was only a matter of time before the team started getting involved. Tweaks were made to everything from side work to scheduling.

A seemingly small but extraordinarily significant idea came from a longtime captain, Kevin Browne.

The baseball-inspired sign language we used to indicate a table's water preference had been so effective, we were always looking for new signs to make our lives easier and the experience better for our guests. Kevin came up with one that changed our culture: if you made eye contact with a colleague and touched your lapel, it meant "I need help."

Before this, asking for help in the middle of a busy service could be challenging. A server would often have to chase their manager across the enormous room; many times, just as they were about to catch up with them, the manager would stop at a table. That meant the server would then have to wait, while their task list continued to pile up. If they were busy enough to need help, spending so much time trying to get it made them even more overwhelmed. Many times, they'd give up and end up back at their station, in a worse position than before they'd tried to get help.

After we introduced Kevin's signal, a server could make eye contact with their manager or one of their colleagues and touch their lapel, and the other person would come help as soon as they could.

It was a small gesture, but the impact it had on the restaurant was not. DBC made it easy to offer help; Kevin gave us an easy way to ask for it.

I believe this sign came to be one of the most important of all of them—and the most long-lived, as I've seen it used in restaurants across the country, disseminated by our alums.

Let's be honest: asking for help is hard, especially for the kind of people who were working at EMP by then—thoroughbreds, accustomed to being the best, who couldn't stand anyone thinking they couldn't handle their workload. In fact, it was often our best people who would get in the most trouble when service was challenging, because they were the ones least likely to ask for help.

Being able to ask for help is a display of strength and confidence. It shows an understanding of your abilities and an awareness of what's happening around you. People who refuse to ask for help, who believe they can handle everything on their own, are deceiving themselves and doing a disservice to those around them. As Danny Meyer used to say, hospitality is a team sport. If you let your ego get in the way of asking for what you need, you're going to let the whole team down, and the hospitality you're delivering is going to suffer.

The sign made it easier and more efficient to ask for help, and systemizing it stripped the stigma from it.

Between slowing down, learning to take a few deep breaths, and finding easy ways to offer and ask for help, this recommitment to balance was crucial. I honestly believe none of the success that came later could have happened without the course correction we made in 2008.

And then, almost as a reward for taking the time to invest in our foundation, the universe (well—Frank Bruni, actually) gave us a little gift.

In December 2008, Bruni gave three stars to Corton in *The New York Times*. Corton was a restaurant Drew Nieporent had opened in Tribeca with the chef Paul Liebrandt. In his review, Bruni said, "Corton is for the most part superb, and joins the constantly improving Eleven Madison Park as a restaurant hovering just below the very summit of fine dining in New York."

We were ecstatic. Buried in this other, unrelated restaurant's review was a secret message to us—*I'm seeing what you've been up to since the last time I visited, and I know you keep getting better.*

Keep going!

CHAPTER 15

THE BEST OFFENSE
IS OFFENSE

The *Michelin Guide* was created at the beginning of the twentieth century as an ingenious marketing ploy. The tire-selling brothers who originated it figured that encouraging people to drive around France to try different restaurants would increase tire sales, so they threw together a free guide of the restaurants in France.

Their star system reflected whether a restaurant was worth traveling for. One star meant a very good restaurant in its category, worth a stop. Two meant excellent cooking, deserving of a detour, while three stood for exceptional cuisine, important enough to merit a special journey.

Over the next century, Michelin, with its secretive team of anonymous inspectors, became the most revered and prestigious restaurant ranking in Europe.

In France, gaining an additional star can make a restaurant's fortunes, while being stripped of one can ruin it: the chef Bernard Loiseau took his own life when it was rumored that his restaurant, La Côte d'Or, was about to lose one of its three stars. (One of the most devastating parts of the story is that the restaurant didn't end up losing the star after all.) So while it may sound like hyperbole to an American, in France, a Michelin star can be a matter of life or death.

The *Michelin Guide* had begun reviewing New York restaurants in 2005. Eleven Madison Park hadn't been on the list then, or in 2006, to no one's surprise. There had been some grumblings in the blogs when we failed to make the list in 2007, but Daniel and I weren't bothered— Michelin is known for moving slowly, and we were still finding our feet.

But in 2008, the buzz was there. We had three stars from the *Times*, and we'd been accepted into Relais & Châteaux, a significant European honor we'd assumed would put us on Michelin's radar. The team was putting 110 percent into every table. So when the New York list was released, we crowded into the office to pore over the announcement.

Le Bernardin had three stars. Jean-Georges had three stars. Masa had three stars. Even the Spotted Pig, April Bloomfield and Ken Friedman's celebrity-filled gastropub, had a star.

We weren't even on the list.

The blow was even more devastating because a restaurant could only increase by one star every year. Not only would we have to wait another year to be included at all, but it would be three years before we could even hope for that coveted third star.

The team was crushed and confused by the snub, and I learned there is no more difficult moment to be the head of a business than when there has been a massive disappointment.

The daily pre-meal meeting meant there was no dodging the discomfort. I was standing in the center of that circle, surrounded by my disheartened friends and colleagues. They were waiting for explanations and comfort, but I had no wand to wave to take the devastation away. All I could do was express my own sadness and confusion, in the hope that sharing the hurt would allow us all to move forward. **A leader's role isn't only to motivate and uplift; sometimes it's to earn the trust of your team by being human with them.**

But I was annoyed by the snub, too, because I knew that we were already pretty freaking excellent and getting better every day. So, after we'd wallowed for a couple of days, I encouraged the team to get mad.

"We've always been at our best when we're the underdogs," I told them at pre-meal, "and here we are again. Think of this as fuel for the fire, and use it." It was time to start playing offense.

Unfortunately, the economy had other plans.

Raindrops Make Oceans

In November 2008, the world was hit by a global recession, which the International Monetary Fund would later call "the most severe economic and financial meltdown since the Great Depression."

To put it mildly: it was not a good time to be selling expensive food.

We got through the holidays okay, but as soon as the New Year turned, business fell off precipitously. The headlines were dire, and cancellations rolled in. We'd started to gain a reputation as a splurge-worthy special-occasion meal, but for most people, it no longer felt prudent to spend so much on a single dinner. Better to dump that money into an emergency fund, a hedge against the worst.

Couples who had gotten engaged at EMP and came back to celebrate with us every year found more frugal ways to celebrate their anniversaries. One couple brought a bottle of champagne to Madison Square Park and raised a glass to our huge windows from across the street—over an order of cheese fries from Shake Shack.

Our private-party business ground to a halt. Wedding parties downsized, either by cutting the guest list or fleeing to more modest venues. And companies, whose lavish private events and cushy expense accounts are a fine-dining restaurant's bread and butter, had switched into austerity mode as well. With fewer deal closings, there were fewer closing celebrations, and if extravagant end-of-year bonuses were still happening, people weren't toasting them in public; suddenly, the optics of a showy, over-the-top, splashed-out dinner felt all wrong.

Most nights, we didn't have enough reservations to seat the whole dining room, so we closed off the area of the restaurant we called Uptown (an area separated from the tables on the lower level by a few steps) to make the empty room feel less cavernous. It was an improvement, and the row of banquettes made for a natural barrier, but you could still tell the restaurant was only half full.

We put on brave faces for our guests, but I spent my nights buried in the books. There was no getting around it: the restaurant's financial situation was desperate and getting worse every day. We had all the expenses associated with running a four-star restaurant without the demand that came with the honor—or the ability to charge four-star prices. So we were hemorrhaging cash. In fact, the only reason we stayed in business was because Eleven Madison Park actually owned Shake Shack at that point in time.

Shake Shack had started in 2004. It was originally a hot dog cart, part of an art installation in Madison Square Park. (When I first arrived at EMP, ShackBurgers were prepped in our private dining room; during lunch service, cooks would walk out the front door of the restaurant carrying giant sheet trays filled with uncooked burgers.) Everybody loved the hot dog stand, and it reopened the next summer, and the next. Eventually, it became Shake Shack, a permanent kiosk serving burgers and frozen custard, modeled after the classic Midwestern roadside shacks of Danny Meyer's youth.

By the time the recession hit, Shake Shack was more than profitable; it was starting to be—well, Shake Shack. The line that snaked around the park had become such a New York institution that Danny bought a webcam, the Shack Cam, so you could gauge the wait from your home or office before deciding whether it was worth coming over.

when it was a brasserie, but if it helped fill those seats and return energy to the dining room, it was worth it.

These inexpensive lunches meant a whole new demographic could suddenly afford us, which bore unexpected dividends. Our goal was to be the four-star restaurant for the next generation, and today's assistant might very well be tomorrow's CEO. The move gave us the opportunity to build and maintain relationships with people who were working their own way up through the ranks.

We made sure guests were getting outrageous value for their twenty-nine bucks (if you're giving a gift, it should be awesome). And in the years that followed, I met countless people who'd been introduced to the restaurant for the first time through those reasonable lunches, some of whom had become our biggest fans.

The recession also had a real adverse impact on check averages. People were just ordering less stuff, and the things they were ordering were less expensive. We obviously couldn't raise prices, so we needed to get creative about how to offset the decrease. This is where things got *really* fun.

When I was a waiter at Tribeca Grill, the rule about delivering dessert was "low and slow"—when walking across the restaurant to deliver desserts to a table, walk more slowly than you ordinarily would as you pass the other tables along the way. And keep that applesauce cake at the guests' eye level, so that by the time you come around with dessert menus, everyone's already been thinking about it. (This is why sugary cereals are always stocked on the lower shelves at the supermarket—it puts them at eye level for kids.)

At EMP, we introduced a dessert trolley—a cart stacked with delicious pies and cakes and tarts—that we could push right over to the table. Most of the time, when you offer people a dessert menu at lunch, they look at you like you're an alien. It's partly calories, but mostly no one has time to go through the whole rigmarole of ordering a dessert, then waiting for it to be plated and brought out and eaten and cleared before they can get the check. Dessert tacks half an hour onto your meal, and at lunch, especially in New York, people are in a hurry to get back to work.

Roll up to their table with a dessert cart, though, and they turn into wide-eyed little kids struggling to choose their treat—especially because they know they can have the one they point at, right away. The cart was beautiful and experiential, and people loved it. Dessert sales went up by 300 percent.

The twenty-nine-dollar lunches brought energy back to the restaurant, even if the margins weren't what we were accustomed to, and a full dining room gave the team the feeling that everything was going to be okay, even when I wasn't completely sure it would be.

More important, the additional business meant we could give the team more hours. We'd spent the past few years hiring an amazing group of people; we couldn't afford to lose them if we wanted to stay the course. As much as they all loved the restaurant and our mission, they had bills to pay. I'm proud to say that we didn't lay off a single member of the team during that time.

Keep the Team Engaged at All Costs

All the cuts we made were having an impact, and all the creative ideas we had come up with to build revenue were as well. But no matter how you spin it, working in austere times is hard. We needed to fully flex our creative muscles—we needed to have some fun. It was time for some 95/5.

Enter the Kentucky Derby.

The year before, a friend had invited me to come down and see his band play at a Kentucky Derby party. The party itself was grubby—more East Village dive bar ironic than the gracious Southern garden party the occasion deserved—but I'd had a blast.

And I loved the idea. The Kentucky Derby! What other occasion has you drinking a signature cocktail in your Easter best? At what other event is it mandatory to wear a fantastic hat? This was a party we could knock out of the park. So, the next spring, we threw ourselves into hosting the most gorgeous, over-the-top Kentucky Derby bash of all time at Eleven Madison Park.

We decorated the room with horse-shaped topiaries, garlanded with roses as if they'd made it to the Winners Circle. The sumptuous buffet featured traditional Southern foods: Benedictine tea sandwiches, fried chicken and waffles, and the meaty braise called Kentucky Burgoo. We had a raw bar and a live band—high-octane American roots bluegrass, courtesy of the Crooners. And our bartenders kept the frosty mint juleps coming in their signature beaded pewter cups.

People love to dress up when they don't have to, and our guests did not disappoint. (We held an informal Best Dressed contest, with the lowest-tech applause-o-meter in history—my own ears.) All this to celebrate the Greatest Two Minutes in Sports, which we watched, breathlessly, on the massive movie screen we'd put up at the back of the restaurant, after a bugler in jodhpurs and a red jacket had sounded the call to post.

The party was a huge risk. Who throws a fancy party in the middle of a recession? But the risk paid off; we broke even. While we didn't make—or lose—money, it did invigorate the team. And we'd partnered with Maker's Mark, Nat Sherman cigars, and *Esquire* magazine, who promoted the event to their own vibrant communities, which broadened ours. A lot of homesick Southerners, horse people, hat lovers, and cigar aficionados were suddenly in love with EMP.

The staff had as much fun at that party as the guests did, and I made a promise to myself: if the restaurant did survive, that sense of playfulness was a quality I never wanted to lose.

We were doing a great job; the experience we were giving our guests was awesome. And we were pinching every penny we could. We'd come up with great ideas to build the brand, and some of them had worked, but the greatest party in the world couldn't compensate for a global recession. Danny was rooting for us, but the bottom line was bleak, and time was running out.

Then, one day at lunch, Frank Bruni walked in.

It Doesn't Have to Be Real to Work

Seeing Frank Bruni saunter in during an otherwise sleepy lunch service incited a rare combination of terror and excitement: obviously, he was there to see whether we deserved another look. We were all way too superstitious to say this out loud, but we couldn't ignore what was true: Bruni would only bother re-reviewing us if he was going to give us four stars.

To be honest, there was quiet chaos in the first moments after his arrival. Nobody burst into tears or broke into a run, but there was some panicked stage-whispering and deer-in-the-headlights moments of forgetting how to walk and talk. Pretty quickly, though, we were able to get past our nerves. And when he left, there were high fives all around: we were confident he'd had a great meal.

Then nothing happened.

Crickets.

Getting reviewed is nuts. In the weeks after the critic comes in, you're on alert. Everything shifts into high gear. Your whole life stops. The chef and the general manager and the wine director stop taking days off; you can't take the chance you won't be there when he comes back.

This is always stressful, but it's tolerable because the period is limited. Critics generally come in three times over a couple of weeks. Then you get the phone call saying that the paper is ready to take pictures, and—for better or worse—it's over.

Except that our review process took months.

Again, just as a mediocre team can't suddenly become great on the day of the Super Bowl, a mediocre restaurant can't become a great one the day the reviewer walks through the door. The restaurant you are is the restaurant they're reviewing, and I stand by that.

But when you're going for four stars, you're aiming for perfection, so we did everything in our power to make his experience perfect—even when he wasn't there. Because every night that Bruni wasn't in the restaurant, which was most of them that year, we designated one random table as the Critic of the Night and used those tables as a dress rehearsal.

These make-believe critics ate at our best table. They were served by our best team and advised on their wine choices by our wine director. When it came time to reset the table for their next course, we didn't pull forks out of a drawer, no matter how meticulously those had been polished before service—no, there was a separate box of silverware set aside, every piece of which had been checked and buffed by a manager. Repolished glasses sat on a separate tray, and every plate for that table was scrutinized for chips and smudges.

The kitchen fired doubles of every dish that the Critic of the Night's table ordered, just as they would when the real critic was in the house, so Daniel could send out whichever one had been ever-so-slightly more perfectly cooked. We assigned our two best food runners to take the food out—two, because you don't want a critic to see the same person over and over again and suspect that you're hand-selecting the people delivering the food to them (which, of course, we were).

It wasn't real, and yet no detail was left to chance.

I thought about this when I watched *The Last Dance*, a documentary about Michael Jordan and the Chicago Bulls, the team he led to six NBA championships. Jordan's competitiveness was legendary; it was his fuel. If another player dared trash-talk him on the court, or to disrespect the Bulls in the media, watch out. But if nobody dared, then Jordan

would fan the flames himself, inventing slights and interpreting acciden-
tal bumps as personal attacks. Any hint of disrespect, even fabricated,
was enough to motivate him to rise to the occasion. He'd create stakes,
even when there were none.

Most nights, the critic in our restaurant wasn't real, just as the rivalry
Michael Jordan created in his head wasn't real, **but it doesn't have to be
real to work**. The ruse was successful.

Were other people in the restaurant getting worse service than the
fake critic? No—in fact, the difference between that table and the one
right next to it would have been completely imperceptible, even if you
knew what to look for; if anything, that level of focus helped us up our
game with every other table. Because the Critic of the Night was for *us*.
It allowed us to role-play so that every single move was rehearsed and
polished to a gleam. It also meant that when Bruni did come in, we'd be so
practiced, not only would there not be any panic, but we would be ready
for him regardless of what table he sat at and what team ended up serving
him. The host would make eye contact and nod, and the cascade would
begin: He's here, and here we go.

Because it took him so long to come back, and because of this unreasonable routine we were running every night, I honestly believe it was in
that year that we finally started operating on a four-star level. Not just
for Frank Bruni, but for everybody else.

In fact, it would be nearly a year between that first lunch and the
eventual review. Even with our confidence and all the practice, the wait
was emotionally trying. I honestly think the only reason we were able to
withstand a review process of that length, especially coupled with our
financial desperation, was because of the cultural reboot we had done. In
short, it was good that we'd figured out how to put our own oxygen
masks on, because there wasn't a lot of relaxation that year.

I eventually forced myself to take a day off to go see *De La Guarda*, a circus-like performance art piece and one of the hottest shows in New York City at the time. It is best known for the ending: after the last, beautiful scene, the music comes up loud, water falls from the ceiling, a confetti cannon goes off, and everyone dances. You leave the theater exhilarated, soaked, and covered in colored paper.

Wouldn't you know it: as soon as I turned my phone back on outside, it buzzed with a missed message: "HE'S HERE!" I left my girlfriend on the corner, sprinted back to my apartment, jumped into the shower, threw on a suit, and was back at the restaurant within thirty-five minutes. I ran into the kitchen, checked in with Daniel, and immediately folded myself into service.

All that practice had paid off. The staff was impeccable and collected—at various points, some of them even looked like they were having fun. This was what we'd been training for. It was time to show him what we could do.

Every fifteen minutes, I'd sneak into a hidden nook next to the barista station with a direct sight line to his table so I could torture myself.

The mind games I played with myself were terrible. I obsessed over every tiny thing that happened, even though I intellectually understood that critics are also human beings and have normal interactions with their friends. I tried to remind myself: if he laughed, he was not cruelly mocking the food. A piece of foie gras left on the plate didn't mean he didn't like it, but that he had been out to dinner six times that week and didn't want to choke down an entire plate of duck liver. Or maybe it did mean he hated it, and everything else we were doing. It was exhausting.

But Bruni seemed to have a good meal that time, too. So we went right back to waiting and practicing and hoping and watching the door.

We spent the rest of that year and the beginning of the next on pins and needles. He came and ate the fall menu and the winter menu. In the summer he came back—again, and again, and again. Then, finally, during the first week of August, we received the call from *The New York Times* to schedule the photographer to shoot the pictures that would accompany our review.

At the *Times*, reviews post online the night before the printed paper is released. So on August 11, 2009, we went into service anxiously awaiting the news.

A group was in the office, refreshing the page over and over again, but I was too nervous to stay in there, so I went back out to the floor, figuring I might as well make myself useful. I was drizzling olive oil tableside over an appetizer of ricotta gnocchi with artichokes when a single diner, one of our regulars, pulled the review up on his phone. He leapt out of his chair, thrust his arm into the air, and yelled, "Four stars!" The whole room erupted in cheers.

I rushed back into the office. Daniel and most of the team were already crowded around the computer, reading the review with giant smiles.

The headline read, "A Daring Rise to the Top." Bruni chronicled our rise from two, to three, and then to four stars, saying that he'd fallen in love "gradually, not all at once." He described watching "an improved, excellent restaurant . . . make yet another unnecessary advance." I couldn't help but see how eerily and accurately those words captured not only the evolution of the guest experience, but the evolution of our culture as well.

That review ended up being his second to last as the critic at *The New York Times*. In his farewell article, he talked about us one last time. In writing about the "wonderful, wonderful meal" he'd had with us, he said, "What I was eating at Eleven Madison Park and what I was feeling in that grand, glorious room added up to a magnitude of enchantment much greater than that at other three-star restaurants."

"A magnitude of enchantment"! We had done it. We had four stars. And we'd earned them through our focus on excellence, but even more so because of our focus on hospitality . . . by being unapologetically us.

But when these less efficient servers were at the tables, connecting with their guests, they were so focused on the interaction that the bonds they created were much stronger. Even if the service was slightly less perfect, the guests liked the experience more.

The first group was attentive; the second paid attention.

I often describe "being present" as caring so much about what you're doing that you stop caring about everything you need to do next. That second group of servers embodied that beautifully. When they were talking to guests, they were *fully present* with them. They were being rewarded for their hospitality, not their excellence.

After EMP earned four stars, my entire focus shifted to hospitality. We had excellence on lock; it was time to double down on relationships. And so, for the next year, being present was our main focus. When we were with a guest, we were *with* that guest. We had trained for years to provide all the starch that people expected from a restaurant of our caliber. Now our focus was on giving those same people more warmth and connection than they expected from a restaurant of our caliber.

We were no longer in the business of running an extraordinary restaurant; we were now in the business of human connection.

And apparently, the world was noticing. Because one morning in early 2010, after I'd checked in with the morning team and made myself a latte, I opened the mail. Bill, junk mail, bill, bill, bill. One envelope piqued my interest, though, and when I ripped it open, I discovered that EMP had been nominated as one of the World's 50 Best Restaurants for 2010.

CHAPTER 17

LEARNING TO
BE UNREASONABLE

I CAN STILL FEEL THE WAVE of embarrassment and disappointment that washed over me when they announced that Eleven Madison Park had come in fiftieth—dead last—on the World's 50 Best Restaurants list for 2010. The twist in my gut is as vivid to me now as it was that night.

I spent the entire flight home from London trying to find the words I would use when I got back to the restaurant and met with the entire team; we knew they'd be devastated by how the awards had turned out for us. Ultimately, it was with my dad's favorite quote that I opened the all-staff meeting Daniel and I led upon our return:

"What would you attempt to do if you knew you could not fail?"

After a setback, it's a leader's job to take their team through their own emotional reckoning—from disappointment to motivation—and to chart the course ahead, because everyone has to be aligned on what you're going to do next.

The restaurant was full; our four stars had made sure of that, and a week before, that had been enough. But Daniel and I had come home from London with a crumpled cocktail napkin and a new goal; we wanted to be the number one restaurant in the world.

"We didn't like hearing our names called in last place; we're going to use that humiliation to push ourselves," we said. "As amazing as the restaurants in the top ten are, we could be just as good, if not better. We want to be number one."

It was a tremendous risk to articulate that dream out loud. When you set a goal for your team and fail to achieve it, you run the risk of damaging morale—and this was a particularly audacious benchmark, given that slipping a single spot would mean falling off the list entirely. But the engine behind that bold statement was another quote, this one by Jay-Z: "I believe you can speak things into existence." I know this for sure: if you don't have the courage to state a goal out loud, you'll never achieve it.

At that meeting, we were inviting the team to decide to go for it with us. When you've surrounded yourself with talented people, there's nothing more powerful than a collective decision. If this electric group decided to accomplish this goal, then—no matter how far-fetched or difficult—we would.

Unsurprisingly, they were on board. We wouldn't have to waste another minute deciding. Now, we just had to do.

Reasonable vs. Unreasonable

When I'd scribbled the words "Unreasonable Hospitality" on that napkin, I hadn't the slightest idea how we'd put those words into practice. But you don't need to know exactly what an idea means to start pursuing it; often, all you need is a sense of what you're trying to achieve. Start pushing, try different things, and the idea will begin to define itself.

Behavioral science expert Rory Sutherland says the opposite of a good idea should also be a good idea. That's why the idea of Unreasonable Hospitality was so compelling. The opposite of Unreasonable Hospitality isn't treating people poorly, it's reasonable hospitality—a perfectly fine way of doing business. But reasonable was not how we were going to become the number one restaurant in the world.

So, we started changing our approach to hospitality in radical ways. Mostly because those words I'd jotted down—Unreasonable Hospitality— gave birth to an idea that would be completely central to everything that came afterward, which was to provide the kind of welcome that would give our guests the feeling we were doing things differently.

We had already upgraded the guest experience, and many of the luxurious details—the creamy linens, the thick leather cover on the wine list, the heft of the silver—were designed to communicate excellence. But we were trying to create a different kind of four-star restaurant, where every detail of your comfort had been anticipated and attended to, one where you felt truly comfortable. And this was where I felt I could make my mark. The details that made us excellent were essential—a dedication to refinement, superior technique, and polish. But I wanted the details that defined our hospitality to be unreasonable.

When we were sitting in the auditorium, waiting for the 50 Best awards to begin, I was aware that every person in the room—Daniel and me included—was engaged in an unreasonable pursuit of excellence. But for almost everyone, the focus of that unreasonable pursuit was what was on the plate. It was the same old story: the magic happened in the kitchen, and the dining room was in service of that magic.

A dish we were known for at the time was a filet of turbot, meticulously covered with paper-thin slices of zucchini arranged to overlap so they mimicked a fish's scales. The fish was then vacuum-packed with olive oil and herbs and cooked sous vide at precisely 54.2 degrees Celsius for eighteen minutes, then served on top of a saffron broth with a fried and stuffed zucchini blossom.

Every single element of the dish represented weeks of research and development and testing; each part took hours of training to prepare and execute. And all for two bites—maybe three minutes of a guest's life!

That's not reasonable, but it's wonderful. I had already seen how impactful our focus on graciousness at EMP had been, so I wondered: What would happen if we took the same unreasonable approach to how we prepared that dish and applied it to hospitality?

Hospitality Isn't a Transaction

We often spoke about the bubble we were working to create around each table.

If the food was timed correctly, the lights and music just right, and our service so complete and unobtrusive that we were always there when the guests wanted us to be, and never when they didn't, then the bubble would exist around every table. Guests wouldn't be distracted by one another; they would be fully engaged in the experience. Time would cease to exist.

But if the food took too long, or if someone dropped a tray of glassware, or if a computer was printing a few feet from their table, then the bubble would pop, and the spell would be broken.

We'd worked hard to make our service flawless, so that the food was perfectly paced and nobody was dropping trays. But as long as that printer was in the dining room, the bubble was getting broken all night long—it was a constant reminder that guests were sitting in our business, not in our home.

I conducted an audit to remove anything that felt transactional from our dining room. We started by banishing the Micros terminals, the computers restaurants use to enter orders and print checks, from the dining room. That was a relatively easy one, though we did have to build a room adjacent to the kitchen, where we could keep them along with the silverware, glassware, and all the other supplies we used for service.

But I saw the biggest opportunity to test-drive Unreasonable Hospitality at our front door, where we welcomed our guests.

Ordinarily, you walk into a restaurant and approach the maître d' standing behind a podium, bathed in the ugly glare of an iPad screen. You say: "Hey, I have a reservation tonight," and give your name. They look down, stab around the screen a little bit. Then the maître d' turns to the host and says, "You can take them to table 23." Everything about that is transactional—the screen, the fact that you're being transported around the restaurant like cargo, the table number.

Maybe I'm being a little dramatic. Certainly, there are plenty of excellent restaurants that handle the exchange elegantly, with warmth and graciousness. But as long as the maître d' is standing behind a podium, a literal barrier between them and the person they are welcoming, the hospitality in that moment can never be more than reasonable. Contrast that with what happens when you go to a friend's house for dinner. They throw open the door, they look you directly in the eyes, and they welcome you by name.

I couldn't help but see an opportunity.

There was some skepticism the first time I sat down with the guest relations team and told them we were going to get rid of the podium at EMP. But if you explain the why along with the what, you'll be surprised how many of these impossible ideas your team can bring to life.

Before long, when guests walked through our doors, instead of having to approach someone who was looking at a screen, they'd be welcomed by name: "Good evening, Ms. Sun—and welcome to Eleven Madison Park." I never tired of seeing the reaction on people's faces when they experienced this for the first time.

Every night, the maître d' would take the list of reservations and Google the names on it, creating a cheat sheet with photos for each seating. If your photo had ever been put on the internet, we would find it— and if you still looked anything remotely like the person in that photo, you would be greeted by name. After the seven thirty reservations were seated, the maître d' would start studying the cheat sheet for the eight o'clock reservations.

Full disclosure: there was still a podium. It was just around the corner from the entrance, so you wouldn't see it when you walked in. Behind that podium was the "anchor," another employee, who was in touch with the dining room and knew whether your table was ready or not. The anchor would communicate in sign language to the maître d', who was effortlessly chatting you up while waiting for instruction; if they signaled that your table was ready, a host would come over and bring you into the dining room. If it wasn't quite ready, the anchor would use a different signal, and the maître d' would usher you into the bar to have a drink while you waited.

None of this was rocket science, but it did require being willing to do whatever it took to bring it to life. What *did* feel like rocket science (to us, at least, based on how challenging it was to execute) was that the maître d' who greeted you was also the person who had confirmed your reservation two days earlier.

At most restaurants, your table is confirmed by a reservationist in an office, gone by the time guests arrive. But we had our maître d's confirm the reservations so that they could start building a relationship before the guests even set foot in the restaurant. So the maître d' could say, "Ms. Sun, my name is Justin; we spoke on the phone the other day. We're so excited to have you with us tonight."

Walking into a fine-dining restaurant like EMP can be intimidating. Being immediately greeted by someone you talked to on the phone a couple of days before made it much less so. And because the real point of those confirmation calls was to learn something about the guest in advance of their arrival and to ask if they were celebrating a special occasion, Justin could also say, "Happy birthday, and thanks for celebrating it with us!"

Obviously, eliminating the podium added steps of service. And besides the Googling and all the nonverbal communication, it took a strategist working the schedule to ensure that the maître d' who'd confirmed your reservation would always be working on the night you came in. For a lot of companies, these extra steps would have been a good reason not to add these flourishes, but I had an Avis car rental tagline from an old commercial stuck in my head: "We try harder."

I have no idea whether that ad was a genuine reflection of the company's culture or some genius on Madison Avenue's way to differentiate one nearly identical car rental service from another, but I thought about the phrase all the time. Isn't that what differentiates the good from the great? Being so committed to an idea that you're willing to try harder, to go to unreasonable lengths in order to bring it to life?

Removing the transactional feeling from the beginning of the meal had such a transformational impact on the experience that I wanted to take it a step further and remove it from the end of the meal as well. If we were now welcoming people more warmly than ever, I wanted our farewell to be just as personal.

"I want to do a ticketless coat check," I told JP Pullos, who was running our front-door team at the time.

"Okay. How?"

"No idea! But you'll come up with something brilliant," I told him. A leader doesn't have to know the details of every plan when they have faith in the people who work for them.

JP did figure it out—and indeed, it was brilliant. He reorganized the regular coat-check room to sort the coats by table number and added an additional, smaller coat check—the "on-deck" coat check—by the door.

During service, a host periodically passed through the dining room, taking note of where people were in their meals so they could plan where they were going to seat the next group of reservations. With our new system, when the host spotted a table paying their check, they'd send someone to transfer the coats from the big coatroom to the on-deck coatroom. By the time the table had finished paying and was heading to the front of the restaurant, we'd be standing by the front door with their coats.

No one was doing this then; very few restaurants do it now. Which is a shame, because it was one of my favorite moments of the night. You'd watch guests approaching the door start to hunt in their pockets or bags for their coat check tags—*where did I put that?* Then they'd look up and recognize their own coat. It was amazing to pull off a magic trick right at the end, blowing the guests' minds one last time; I never got tired of seeing it.

Hospitality Is a Dialogue, Not a Monologue

It is impossible to get a reservation at Rao's.

Rao's, which opened in 1896 and serves homestyle Italian American food in Harlem, is a New York institution. And when I say it's impossible to get a reservation there, I mean it: they don't take them. A select few people "own" tables, and you can't eat there unless you're invited by someone who does.

After years of asking everyone I knew, I finally managed to wrangle myself an invitation. The meal was amazing (the meatballs are some of the best I have ever had). And while the dining experience was pretty removed from the one we were trying to provide, it made a big impression on me.

There weren't any menus at Rao's; instead, a guy called Nicky the Vest pulled a barstool up to our table and told us our options. We didn't hear about the pastas until we'd picked our antipasti; we didn't hear about meat until we'd picked our pastas. It was a conversation—or felt like one, though you somehow always ended up eating what Nicky thought you should eat.

I loved it. It was like going to my grandma's house for dinner, and I left convinced we should get rid of our menus altogether.

After the evening's wine was out of my system, I realized we weren't ready for quite so radical a move. (Later, we would be.) But I was entranced by the idea that ordering your meal could take the form of a back-and-forth exchange between the restaurant and the guest. Danny Meyer says that hospitality is a dialogue, not a monologue. He meant it metaphorically, but I wanted to make the dialogue literal.

For years, we'd offered both a prix fixe menu and a chef's tasting menu. The prix fixe gave the guest control; the tasting menu afforded surprise.

I wanted a less binary option. There was charm in the unexpectedness and flow—the narrative—of a tasting menu, but it was also a directive, subjecting the diner to a monologue from the kitchen: "This is what you're going to eat tonight."

As you may have gathered by now, I like to be in control. That's especially true at dinner, because I'm a bit of a picky eater: I don't like fishy fish or organ meats. And as someone who loves food, I like to determine not only what I don't want to eat on a given night, but what I do.

We came up with a new menu idea, which would encompass the best of both worlds. On a normal menu, all your options are listed in their entirety: the beef comes with potato puree and chanterelle mushrooms. You decide exactly what you want, and you get exactly what you order. With many tasting menus, on the other hand, there's no menu at all; you find out what you're going to be eating when the plate is put down in front of you.

The beauty of the former is control; the beauty of the latter is surprise. Our new menu captured both.

We listed our dishes only by their principal ingredient; on a given night, say, your choice of entrée might be between beef, duck, lobster, or cauliflower. You controlled which of those you ordered but got to enjoy the surprise of how the ingredient was prepared and served when it was delivered.

Daniel loved the new menu format because it gave him flexibility—if a vendor surprised him with a few boxes of gorgeous sorrel or special summer beans, he could incorporate those without reprinting a hundred menus. I loved it because it necessitated a conversation. As Oliver Strand wrote in his aptly titled article in *The New York Times* about the menu change, "At Eleven Madison Park, Fixing What Isn't Broke": "The menu is almost an abstraction. Rather than seducing you with luscious descriptions, it's a reason—or provocation—to talk to your server about what you feel like eating."

A few months after we launched the new menu, I had a meal at Momofuku Ssäm Bar, which encouraged me to push this idea of dialogue and choice even further. There was a small box in the lower right-hand corner of Ssäm Bar's menu that read: "No substitutions or special requests. We do not serve vegetarian-friendly items."

Wait, what? I have nothing but admiration for what chefs do, and I know some substitutions will destroy the integrity of a dish. But from a hospitality perspective, that blanket statement—no accommodations, no matter what—was shocking and went against everything I believed in. (It's worth noting that in the years since, Momofuku's owner, David Chang, has become more flexible and one of the most hospitable chefs I know.)

But that night, I couldn't keep my eyes off that box and ended up journaling about it over my nightly glass of red wine. How can a restaurant tell someone who doesn't want meat that they have to have it if they want to eat there? What we were doing with the new menu format was all well and good, as far as what the guest wanted—but were we doing enough to give the guest a voice about what they *didn't* want?

At the time we, like every other restaurant, would ask the guest at the beginning of the meal if they had any allergies. But not killing your guests is table stakes; surely we could do better? What if we also asked them if there were any ingredients they didn't like? Or if there was anything they just weren't in the mood to eat that night? Now *that* would be a proper dialogue.

It took a bit of convincing to get Daniel and the kitchen staff on board with this one, as they would have to do most of the heavy lifting, coming up with endless variations on dishes they'd already perfected. If the chicken was served with asparagus and morels but the guest didn't like mushrooms, the kitchen would need to have an alternate but equally delicious preparation of the chicken prepped and on hand, just in case. It was the very definition of unreasonable. But Daniel could see how revolutionary the idea was, if we could bring it to life. (I also pulled the "This is important to me" card.)

We decided to give it a shot. And it nearly didn't work at all.

A couple of weeks after we'd started asking diners about their preferences, not one single table had told us about an ingredient they didn't like. I took a station to see if I could figure out why.

There is, by the way, no better way for a leader to figure out why an idea isn't working—or how it can work better—than to walk a mile in the shoes of the people you've charged with implementing that idea. In general, this is good practice. If you're the CEO of a hotel chain, work the front desk at one of your hotels a couple of times a year; if you run an airline, take a shift at the ticket desk, or serve drinks and pretzels in economy. Not ceremonially, either—do the job. I bet you'll be surprised by what you learn; I always was.

My serving skills were a little rusty, and the people supporting me had to work harder than they would have if the team had been headed by a competent captain. But it took only a few tables before I knew what the problem was.

At the time, Andrew Zimmern and Anthony Bourdain were all over TV, eating still-beating cobra hearts, fetal ducks from unhatched eggs, and soups made from silkworm larvae. Every high-end menu featured ingredients—treviso! 'nduja! cardoon!—obscure enough that even a seasoned diner might need to Google them under the table.

If you were someone who cared about food, which most of our guests were, the trend was to eat widely and indiscriminately. So it wasn't cool to admit that the texture of eggplant or caviar grossed you out or that you hated beets because your mom had served the slimy ones from the can. And if you weren't going to confess those things to your nearest and dearest, you certainly weren't going to unburden yourself to the captain at a four-star restaurant.

So the next time I asked the question, I made my own (true) confession: I told the guests how I feel about sea urchin. Sea urchin is rare and difficult to source. It is a delicacy many sophisticated eaters love: creamy and decadent, beloved by chefs. And the mere thought of it makes me want to puke.

Sure enough, once I'd come clean, the guy in seat two said, "Actually, I'm not crazy about oysters," and his wife said, "Yeah, I hate celery."

It wasn't until I'd shown myself to be vulnerable that the people I was serving allowed me to see their vulnerability. Is it an expression of vulnerability to say you don't like an ingredient? I think it is—and the more open you demonstrate yourself to be, the more likely people are to be open with you.

In that moment, for me, the new menu format was a true success. We'd turned what had been a one-way conversation into a genuine exchange.

Treat Everyone Like a VIP

Personal training sessions with a celebrity trainer. A three-night stay at a lighthouse on the coast of Sweden. Twenty-five thousand dollars' worth of services from a Park Avenue dermatologist. A lifetime supply of luxury face cream. A Tiffany crystal-studded cat collar. A year of complimentary Audi rentals. A ten-day walking tour of Japan.

We weren't the first people to be unreasonable in our approach to hospitality, but that kind of over-the-top service had always been limited to a select few: celebrities, politicians, the wealthy and elite. Think of the exorbitant gift bags Oscar nominees famously get every year. (See partial list above.)

For us, Unreasonable Hospitality meant providing thoughtful, high-touch gestures for every one of our guests.

Our first pass at leveling the playing field came in our reimagining of the kitchen tour. Many fine-dining restaurants have chef's tables, but it had always bugged me that only one table got to experience a meal at that table every night; even at EMP, visits to the kitchen had always been reserved for the biggest VIPs. But if we believed holistically in the concept of Unreasonable Hospitality, we needed the most gracious elements of the experience to be available to everyone.

We created a nook in our kitchen with an expansive view of the thirty precision-trained cooks working with laser focus and in near silence in our enormous, immaculate kitchen, and put a chef's table in that nook. But our chef's table had no chairs; our guests stood while enjoying a single course.

Because it was only a single course, we could offer that special experience to *lots* of people—everyone who showed interest in experiencing it. (This course was neutral—never a dessert—so it could happen at any point in the meal; the first one we did was a liquid nitrogen cocktail.) We even hired someone whose only job was to give those tours. Not everyone wanted to see the kitchen; some people had come to the restaurant to negotiate a deal, or to stare passionately into each other's eyes, or simply to eat—and the staff was tuned in enough to leave those folks alone. But for everyone else—whether you were Jay-Z and Beyoncé, or a couple who had saved up so you could experience a four-star restaurant for the first time, the experience was yours to have.

What's the Hospitality Solution?

The very end of the meal is always precarious from a hospitality perspective. First of all, it's time to pay, and that's never fun. The cold, hard reality of those numbers on a check can throw cold water on the magical vibe you've built over the course of the evening.

And the timing is hard to get right. When some guests are ready to leave, they're ready to leave. People get impatient (*I* get impatient!) if the process of getting the check, paying it, and getting out the door takes too long. But at the same time, you can never put the check down before the guest has asked for it, because that gives them the feeling you're trying to rush them out.

At EMP, we used hospitality to solve both potential problems. We didn't wait for the guest to ask for the check. Instead, at the end of their meal, we'd bring the bill over and drop it off—along with an entire bottle of cognac.

We'd pour everyone at the table a splash and leave the full bottle on the table: "Please, help yourself to as much as you like, with our compliments. And when you're ready, your check is right here."

People were delighted by this. The ability to pour for themselves felt even more luxurious and surprising to them after a three-hour meal where they hadn't had to lift a finger, and that was the feeling I was trying to replicate: the moment, at the end of a dinner party, when a guest leans forward, grabs the mostly empty bottle of wine left on the table, and tops off everyone's glass.

But more important, there's no way a person who has just been given a full bottle of free booze can feel like they're being rushed out. And yet, at the same time, the check was right there whenever they were ready for it. We no longer had to "drop the check" on one of our guests, and they would never have to ask for it again.

This is a hospitality solution: a problem that we solved not by sneakily chipping away at the service we were offering but by blowing it out in the opposite direction—by giving more, not less.

Too often, when we're faced with a pernicious problem in our businesses, we fall back on the tried-and-true: push harder, be more efficient, cut back. Especially when the problems are nagging ones that erode the bottom line or those that persist because our organizations rely on humans and all their wonderful and fallible ways.

Imagine, though, that instead of resorting to one of these fallback positions, you asked yourself: What is the hospitality solution? What if you forced yourself to be creative, to develop a solution that worked because of—not in spite of—your dedication to generosity and extraordinary service?

These are almost always harder to execute, and coming up with them will definitely call on your creative side. But they're almost always a win. If a stumble at the end of a meal can undo all the goodwill a restaurant has earned in the three hours preceding it, then a gorgeous, gracious gesture at the end can have the opposite effect. (This is true in every service industry.)

And while dropping off a full bottle of expensive booze at every table seemed like an unreasonably extravagant gesture, it was actually cost-effective. After an elaborate multicourse dinner (and usually plenty of wine), few people were interested in drinking more than a sip of that cognac. Yet the feeling of abundance was there.

CHAPTER 18

IMPROVISATIONAL HOSPITALITY

ONE AFTERNOON, I WAS CLEARING the appetizer plates from a four-top of Europeans headed straight to the airport after their meal.

A quick aside: there's nothing more flattering than a guest walking into the restaurant with luggage. It means they've chosen you to be either their first or last meal in New York—their first or last memory of the city. It's an enormous compliment, and a responsibility I don't take lightly.

Another aside: I bussed a lot of tables when I was general manager. At that point, it didn't make sense for me to take an order; the captains and sommeliers were more qualified to walk guests through the food on the menu and to offer suggestions for wine. Bussing tables showed the team I was there to help and gave me a way to check in with tables without worrying they'd ask a question I didn't have a good answer for.

Anyway! As I was clearing this particular table, I overheard the four guests crowing about the culinary adventures they'd had in New York: "We've been everywhere! Daniel, Per Se, Momofuku, now Eleven Madison Park. The only thing we didn't eat was a street hot dog."

If you'd been in the dining room that day, you'd have seen an animated bulb appear over my head, like in a cartoon. I dropped the dirty dishes off in the kitchen and ran out to buy a hot dog from Abraham, who manned the Sabrett's cart on our corner.

Then the hard part: I brought the hot dog back to the kitchen and asked Daniel to plate it.

He looked at me like I'd gone crazy. I was always trying to push the boundaries, but serving what New Yorkers call a dirty-water dog at a four-star restaurant? I held my ground and told him to trust me—that it was important to me—and he finally agreed to cut the hot dog into four perfect pieces, adding a swoosh of mustard, a swoosh of ketchup, and perfect quenelles of sauerkraut and relish to each plate.

Before we brought out their final savory course, I admitted to the guests that I'd been eavesdropping: "We're thrilled you chose us for your last meal in New York, but we didn't want you to go home with any culinary regrets," I said, as the kitchen servers set the artistically plated hot dog sections down at each place.

They *freaked out.*

I had given away thousands of dishes, and many, many (many) thousands of dollars' worth of food by that point in my career, and yet I can confidently say that nobody had ever responded the way that table responded to that hot dog. In fact, before they left, each person at the table told me it was the highlight not only of the meal, but of their trip to New York. They'd be telling the story for the rest of their lives.

Athletes go to the tape when they've had a bad game, to see what they can fix. They don't often go to the tape when they've had a great game—but that's how you celebrate and hold on to what you did well. So I started talking to the staff in pre-meal about the hot dog: What had made the gift so good? And what about it could we systemize?

Find the Legend

One of Spago's best regulars ate lunch there five days a week. Physically, he was a huge man, and ordinary restaurant chairs can be uncomfortable for someone that big. So when they opened the new Spago in Beverly Hills, Barbara Lazaroff, Wolfgang Puck's wife at the time and a tremendous creative force in the company, asked the regular's wife to secretly photograph and measure his favorite chair at home. She then had a furniture maker replicate it and upholster the new chair in the house fabric.

This gesture made an impression on me—and not just because it was my job to move this enormous custom-made chair from the back of the restaurant to the regular's table every single morning the summer I worked there. Though I wasn't using this language at the time, I can say now that I loved that gesture because it was unreasonable. I *still* get a kick out of imagining the look on the regular's face the first time he saw his chair.

Having a piece of furniture custom-made for a regular goes way above and beyond ordinary service; it is extreme thoughtfulness and inclusion and generosity. More important, though, it's one-off hospitality—the same reason the hot dog was a hit.

It's fun to hear a band play the songs you already love, but it's even more wonderful when they start improvising and you know that only the people in *this* room, on *this* night, will ever hear this particular version. (This is why Grateful Dead fans trade bootleg copies of their favorite Red Rocks shows; no two are alike.)

And I wanted to improvise, one guest at a time. Everyone at our restaurant on a given night was sharing a unique experience—but what if everyone in the restaurant could have their own unique experience? With the new menu, we'd given our guests the gift of choice. Now, I wanted to give as many of them as possible the gift of delight—the surprise that comes from being truly seen and heard.

The chair at Spago, which probably cost Barbara a few thousand dollars, may have been inspiring, but it wasn't scalable; we couldn't do that for everyone who came in, or even for a select few. But the hot dog was proof that we didn't have to call in a furniture maker to blow someone's mind. All we had to do was pay attention.

Over the next month or so, we started to play around with ways we could make some of these magical moments happen. When a table spent the better part of their meal talking about a movie they'd loved and forgotten about, we dropped off a DVD of it (remember those?) with their check. A couple celebrating an anniversary mentioned they were staying at a nearby hotel; we made sure there was a bottle of champagne waiting for them in their room when they got back, along with a handwritten note thanking them for trusting us with such an important occasion.

A four-top of parents debating the ethics of the Tooth Fairy found a quarter under their folded napkins every time one of them returned from the bathroom. We finished a meal for someone who told us they loved Manhattans with a flight of variations on that cocktail—the Perfect Manhattan, so-called not because it improves on the original but because it uses equal amounts of both sweet and dry vermouths; the Brooklyn, made with the French aperitif Amer Picon; the Distrito Federal, which substitutes aged tequila for the bourbon.

We were getting real traction with the guests as a result of these little gestures, and the staff was on fire coming up with ever-cooler tricks we could pull. We'd unlocked something important, and we wanted to do it all the time. The only problem was a big one: we didn't have the personnel. There isn't a group of people standing around behind the scenes at a busy restaurant twiddling their thumbs and waiting for an errand to run, and we certainly couldn't risk compromising the impeccable service we were known for by pulling necessary people off the floor.

If we were going to commit to this, we needed to create a position.

Christine McGrath was a host and reservationist, as well as a skilled calligrapher. Since handwritten notes were a big part of what we were doing in those early days, we were already stealing her from her duties on a regular basis. She was the obvious person to step into the role full-time. I hired an additional host to free her up, and just like that, we had a designated person in place to execute our ideas—Eleven Madison Park's first official Dreamweaver.

I named the position after the iconic song by Gary Wright, which has always had a special place in my heart because it was playing the first time I kissed a girl. (It will now be in your head for the rest of the day—sorry.)

Sure enough, appointing Christine meant we were able to make these moments happen more frequently and more consistently. Meanwhile, I was still wondering how we could do more. Then one night, I was dining at Danny Meyer's pizza place Marta. Our server was a woman named Emily Parkinson, who confessed that she was fangirling extra hard over our table because she'd had such a wonderful solo meal at Eleven Madison Park.

Then she mentioned she'd painted her meal.

At first, I thought I'd misheard her. But while most people take pictures of their food, Emily *paints* hers. Actually, she made preliminary pencil sketches of each course while she was at the restaurant; later, she finished the drawings with a watercolor wash.

Charmed, I asked her to send me some photos, and the next morning, her illustrations were in my inbox. (You can see them, too; *Grub Street* did a piece on Emily, featuring the paintings she made of her meal at EMP.) I'd barely opened the email before I'd picked up the phone to call my friend Terry Coughlin, the GM of Marta: "Tell me right away if this is a nonstarter, but I'm working on something pretty cool over here and I want to poach Emily to help me with it. . . ."

Emily's artistic talent supercharged the program. She'd run with whatever wild idea you brought her. A watercolor portrait of their new home in the country for a couple leaving New York to start a family? Done. A three-foot-tall AT-AT wine decanter for a Star Wars superfan who also happened to be a wine geek? No problem. And her flawless execution of these ideas made the team even more ambitious.

Before long, we had multiple Dreamweavers on staff, working in their own fully equipped studio. (We set them up in the reservationist's office—I told you everything gets stashed in there!) It was Santa's workshop, complete with leather punching and metalworking tools, a sewing machine, and every art supply you can imagine. And we weren't shy about putting it all to good use.

In the years to come, Emily and the team would paint a pastoral scene, complete with cows and ducks, so a visiting chef known for hunting much of the protein at his restaurant could choose his entrée by shooting it with a Nerf gun during his kitchen tour.

A captain overheard one of our out-of-town regulars regretting he hadn't gotten his daughter a stuffed animal as he'd promised, so Emily fashioned a perfect little teddy bear for him out of kitchen towels.

A couple came in, splurging on dinner to console themselves after their vacation flight was canceled. We turned the private dining room into a private beach, complete with beach chairs, sand on the ground, and a kiddie pool filled with water they could stick their toes into, and they drowned their disappointment in tropical daiquiris decorated with little umbrellas.

When a couple who'd gotten married at EMP came to celebrate their anniversary, we invited them to eat dessert at a table we'd set up in the private dining room where they were married. The room was set with flowers, candles, a champagne bucket—the whole nine—and as they were finishing their dessert, we turned the lights even lower and hit play on "Lovely Day" by Bill Withers—their wedding song, a detail we'd found in our notes. Then we turned the lights a little lower and closed the door behind us.

We were already Googling guests so we could greet them by name. That preliminary research became an important pipeline. A gentleman coming in for his birthday had a popular Instagram account devoted to his love of bacon; I asked the pastry chef to create a bacon granola for him instead of our customary coconut-pistachio. We created an ice-cream course with every outrageous sundae topping you can imagine (and some only a brigade of highly skilled cooks could bring to life) for a guest who had an Instagram account dedicated to her love of the cone.

These people were having experiences they couldn't have anywhere else—and many of them were having experiences no other table in the restaurant was having. It was like the Dead giving every fan their own show; at EMP, you would have needed forty bootleg cassettes to capture a single night.

One night, a banker hustling to fund a new company teased his captain: sure, an after-dinner drink would be great, but what he *really* needed was a million dollars to finish his raise. Alas, our budget only stretched to a bag filled with ten 100 Grand chocolate bars, which we tucked under his chair.

When he was done laughing, he told us his night at the restaurant had been "legendary." I told the story in pre-meal, and the term "Legend" became shorthand within the restaurant for these special touches—as in, "I did the best Legend for a table last night."

The name took on even greater significance as we realized what made these Legends so legendary. Namely, they gave people a story—a Legend—to tell.

Why do people put so much time and effort into a marriage proposal? Because they know it's a story they'll tell for the rest of their lives. The best of those stories do two things: First, they put you right back in the moment, so that you're not just recounting the experience, but reliving it. Second, the story itself tells you that while you were having the experience, you were seen and heard.

These days, people, especially younger people, are more interested in collecting experiences than in getting more stuff. But restaurant meals, like many service experiences, are ephemeral. You can take a copy of the menu home, and pictures of your plate, but you can't relive that bite of foie gras.

That changes when you leave with a story that's good enough to put you back in the moment, as if you were living it all over again. That's why we took the Legends so seriously. If people were coming to us to add to their collection of experiences, then we saw these not as extra flourishes but as a responsibility: to give people a memory so good it enabled them to relive their experience with us.

The true gift, then, wasn't the street hot dog or the bag full of candy bars; it was the *story* that made a Legend a legend.

Giving More Is Addictive

The energy around these extra grace notes—these Legends—was phenomenal.

The dining room team was magnificent at what they did, and they were passionate about what they were doing. But no matter how much you love your job, the same thing night after night gets stale.

In restaurants, it's usually the people in the kitchen who get to explore their creativity—whether collaborating with the chef on a new dish or feeding their colleagues at family meal (trust me, you will hear about it if the family meal you put up is no good). With the Legends, everyone in the dining room had an outlet, too—they weren't just serving plates of other people's creativity; they had the opportunity to infuse the experience with their own.

The Legends—whether you were watching other people do one or doing them yourself—made coming to work fun, and we were working way too hard not to have fun. I even started a private Instagram account to catalog them, so that if you'd missed one on your day off, you could still be encouraged and inspired. And we celebrated every single one in pre-meal.

If you *were* the person behind a Legend, you immediately wanted to find a way to do another. Seeing that look of wonder and delight cross a guest's face as they realized what they were seeing was a transformational moment; as soon as you'd had that feeling, you wanted it again.

The guests weren't the only ones to benefit, either, because when one of our own came in to dine, we pulled out all the stops.

It's worth mentioning that at the time some famous, old-school fine-dining restaurants didn't permit staff to dine in at their restaurants at all. The rationale was that if a guest sat next to someone who had previously served them, it would degrade the experience somehow. After all, nobody wants to sit next to the help—right?

This makes me furious. The only thing a rule like this does is tell the people who work so tirelessly for you that's all they are: the help.

We went hard in the other direction. Eliazar Cervantes loved mariachi—so of course a band of musicians emerged from the walk-in and serenaded him during his tour. When Jeff Tascarella, the general manager at the NoMad, warned us in advance that his dad was more of a Budweiser steak-and-potatoes guy than Sauternes and foie, we transformed our champagne cart into a Budweiser cart.

One of our senior dining room captains, Natasha McIrvin (who would later go on to be our creative director) is completely obsessed with Christmas. The first year she didn't go home for the holiday, her parents came to New York to surprise her; we hid them in the walk-in. When the family had reunited and returned to their table, they found a snowy, holiday-themed train on a tiny track circling golden reindeer, pine garlands, and a giant pile of beautifully wrapped gifts. This was our caviar course—everything bagels balanced on top of the train cars, and a tin of caviar and all the trimmings hidden in the presents beneath the wrapping and bows.

Over the top? You bet. Not only did we want our people to come in for dinner; we wanted them to have a better experience than anyone else in the room. It was a way to say thank you for all that the team gave us—their creativity, good humor, and hard work. But it was also to show them the same graciousness they delivered every day. What better way to get fired up about giving Unreasonable Hospitality than to spend an evening receiving it?

I often wonder why more companies don't invest in their own people this way. Major banks have private wealth managers, who deliver a heightened level of service to their wealthiest clients. How much would it cost to give every teller a similarly attentive private banking experience? Wouldn't that make sense from a retention standpoint? And perhaps more important, how can you even quantify the improvement in the kind of service someone will deliver to their customers when they have themselves received the very best the bank has to offer?

For us, it was an ideal investment. The Dreamweaver idea may have originated with me, but it was the team who breathed life into it every day. The best part for me was scrolling through that private Instagram account and seeing idea after idea I'd had *nothing to do with*. I hadn't conceived of the concepts; I hadn't approved them. The team had come up with them independently and executed them so brilliantly that even I was inspired by them.

It was the perfect marriage of ownership and improvisational hospitality.

Create a Tool Kit

I hear this a lot: "Well, of course you could afford to pull those tricks at an expensive restaurant."

And I always think: *Are you sure you can afford* not *to?*

It's true—these gifts cost money, in labor if nothing else. But I'm my dad's son, and I reviewed the Dreamweaver line item in the P&L every month with an eagle eye. There was never any question: given the word-of-mouth marketing this bought us with our guests and the excitement this kind of gift-giving created among the team, the program was worth every penny.

Anyway, as a leader, you can't rely solely on your spreadsheets. You have to trust your gut—and what you feel when you're in the room with people, giving and receiving these gifts. Is there a traditional return on investment with a program like this? No. Am I confident that each dollar I spent here did as much or more than the ones I spent on traditional marketing? Absolutely.

In many ways, it was the perfect example of the Rule of 95/5 in action: we could afford to splurge on Legends because we were managing our money so closely the rest of the time. But most of the time, we didn't have to break the bank to blow someone's mind: we'd put ten drugstore candy bars in a bag, and a guest had called us legendary for it!

It isn't the lavishness of the gift that counts, but its pricelessness.

I'd learned the importance of this in high school, when I worked as a busser and host at the Ruth's Chris Steak House in the Westchester Marriott. That Ruth's Chris was a franchise, and so it had to closely follow the guidelines of the parent company: the same signage, uniforms, china, glass, silver; the same menu.

But the one I worked for had a secret: a fried calamari dish that wasn't on the menu.

Every piece of fried calamari I'd ever had before had been cut into rings. This calamari was cut into strips. And I have no idea what they breaded it with, but it was flipping *delicious*. (Yes, I ate the leftovers off the tables I bussed. Absolutely disgusting. I have no regrets.)

You couldn't order this calamari; you could only get it if they sent it out to you. Often, when you're a regular (or if a restaurant messes up your order and wants to get back into your good graces), they'll send you an extra appetizer, or a dessert, or a glass of champagne. The problem is that you know exactly how much that dessert cost: "Oh, they love me fourteen dollars' worth." But you could only get the fried calamari if you were part of the club—or if someone wanted you to feel like you were. The cost to the restaurant was insignificant; its impact was not.

That calamari was, by definition, priceless, just like the two-dollar street hot dog I'd sent to that table. But it was also right there, every night—a gift waiting to be given. Sending this priceless calamari didn't require planning or strategy; all it took was an impulse and the press of a button.

This is an important strategy for every business. Improvisational hospitality is fundamentally reactive. You're always responding—either to the information that you've gathered in advance (a guest telling the reservationist they're coming in to celebrate his wife's fortieth) or to a tidbit you've overheard at the table.

But, as oxymoronic as it may seem, you can also be proactive about improvisational hospitality. This is simple pattern recognition: **identify moments that recur in your business, and build a tool kit your team can deploy without too much effort.**

Brainstorm materials it would be useful to have on hand, organize those materials on-site so that staff can readily access them, and empower the people who work for you to use them. Do that, and you've systemized improvisational hospitality.

We had done this for years at EMP with what we called the Plus One cards. (We did these for so long I genuinely can't remember if we started them or if they predated me.) Plus One cards were answers to questions we were frequently asked—Who does your floral arrangements? Can you tell me more about the farm that made this cheese?—printed on simple index cards we kept in a card catalog box in the back. If a server saw a guest flip a plate to see who'd made it, they brought the card that explained who Jono Pandolfi was and where you could see more of his work.

We called them Plus One because they were a little extra. Unnecessary, but nice to have. Guest expectations for us were high by that point, and this was a way for us to overdeliver—to give a little bit more, even, than what they were expecting. And because they were printed up, filed neatly, and ready to go, it took little effort for the staff to take advantage of them.

There are two kinds of people: the kind who love to receive gifts, and the kind who love to give them. To be clear, both are equally selfish, because people who love to give gifts get their own reward when they see the amazed look that tells them they've nailed it.

By the time the Dreamweaver program was in full swing, the people who were working for us tended to fall into the camp of people who loved to give gifts, and they were *great* at delivering Legends. But we wanted to make sure they had the opportunity to give all the time, not just when they had a moment of inspiration, so we created a tool kit.

Since people visiting from out of town often asked about our own favorite haunts in the city, we printed little maps, marked with some of our secret spots: the best pizza slice, the best bagel, the best place to get Sunday brunch, along with lesser-known New York City treasures like the Rubin Museum. We bought tickets to the observation deck of the Empire State Building we could give out to tourists who were super excited to be in New York. (I know tons of born-and-bred New Yorkers who have never gone up there because it seems cheesy—and it is, but it's also an *amazing* way to see the city. Smuggle a flask.)

As our focus on Unreasonable Hospitality grew, we were always looking for a way to "plus one" the experience—to give people a little more than they expected—by staying alert to recurring situations.

People often slipped outside for a cigarette during their meal; while they were out there, we'd bring them a splash of booze in a little to-go cup we'd special-ordered for the purpose.

Another, and probably my favorite: when a couple got engaged at the restaurant, we would pour them complimentary glasses of champagne, like every restaurant does. But their champagne flutes were different than all the others in the dining room—they were crystal flutes I'd partnered with Tiffany to provide. At the end of their meal, we'd send the couple home with a gift box in that iconic robin's-egg blue, containing the glasses they'd used for their engagement toast. The partnership was an easy win for Tiffany; I guarantee most of those couples put a full set of flutes onto their registries.

And it was a lovely win for us.

As the Dreamweavers built up some steam, many of the items they created as bespoke presents or Legends became part of our tool kit.

One afternoon, a table laughed with their captain about overdoing it with the wine and wished out loud that instead of going back to the office, they could head home for a tipsy nap. So the Dreamweaver sent them out with a wink—a fake doctor's note excusing them for the afternoon, and a pack of aspirin.

But people often made a similar joke: "Oof, we went *hard* tonight; tomorrow's gonna hurt!" So the Dreamweavers put together a little morning rescue kit—a bag of strong ground coffee, some Alka-Seltzer tablets, and a muffin—for the captains to hand out whenever a guest anticipated their hangover out loud.

And because the Dreamweavers were standing by, a captain might say, "I loved that impromptu snack box you put together for the woman who was catching the red-eye to Seattle. I would love to be able to give those out on a more frequent basis; could we make a bunch?"

Then those airplane snack boxes were just *there*, waiting for a traveler to check bags because they'd be leaving straight from lunch to the airport. At the end of their meal, we'd hand them their coat, roll out their luggage—oh, and when you get hungry again on the plane, here's a nicer nosh than a pack of stale pretzels.

The fresh elements had to be baked and restocked daily, but the thinking—the idea, the plan, the basic execution—had to happen only once. Prepare for these recurring moments in advance, and your staff doesn't have to reinvent the wheel every night—they just have to listen and make it happen.

You might be wondering: Once you've systemized it, is it still hospitable? Does that airplane snack box carry the same warmth and generosity the thirtieth time you hand one to a guest as it did the first? After all, we're talking about bespoke hospitality—is something lost if the gift isn't specific to you?

Without hesitation, I can say no, because **the value of a gift isn't about what went into giving it, but how the person receiving it feels.** Maybe it was the thirtieth time we'd handed a traveling guest a snack box, but *it was the first time for them*—and their delight wasn't dimmed in the slightest because they hadn't been the only ones.

We were always looking for ways to scale what was unique—and working—about what we were offering, and counterbalancing those gestures with one-off, improvisational hospitality.

It was important to keep checking in with the systems we had put in place to make sure they hadn't started to feel expected or formulaic or outgrown their usefulness. But in general, systemizing these gestures made it possible to make more people happy. And the team could use the leftover bandwidth to focus on the more singular moments—to create those Legends.

Opportunities for Hospitality Exist in Every Business

One of my close friends runs one of the big realty firms in New York and has asked me on a couple of occasions to talk to her team about hospitality. The first thing I ask the real estate agents is what gift they leave to welcome a new homeowner. Ninety-nine percent of the time, they tell me, "A bottle of sparkling wine in the fridge."

Now, a bottle of bubbles is nothing to complain about. But there's also nothing personal, nothing inspiring or memorable, about it—and there should be!

You're selling someone a home or helping them to sell the one they've lived in. That's one of the most intimate transactions there is. For the amount of time that an agent spends with people, listening to their hopes and dreams for the future (incidentally, much longer than I've ever spent with a table), and the size of the average commission, a real estate professional should absolutely be able to figure out a bespoke gift for everyone they work with.

Again: not expensive, necessarily, but personalized. That hot dog cost two dollars, but there was probably only one table in the history of the restaurant that I could have presented it to. People often confuse hospitality with luxury, but I could have given that table a bottle of vintage Krug and a kilo of caviar, and it wouldn't have had anywhere near the same impact. **Luxury means just giving more; hospitality means being more thoughtful**.

So: if your buyer is into music, leave them their favorite album on vinyl—and, depending on the size of your commission, spring for a turntable as well. If a client dreamed out loud about doing yoga in that nook off the hallway with the sunlight streaming through, then buy a mat and roll it out there, so it's the first thing to greet them when they walk into their new home.

A yoga mat doesn't take any more time, energy, or resources to secure than a bottle of Prosecco, just a bit more thoughtfulness.

Many good businesspeople make these gestures instinctively. A real estate agent I spoke to told me about a Legend she'd pulled, long before she knew the term. Since she knew the new owners were planning a gut renovation, she got permission to remove the doorjamb where her client, the seller, had marked her kids' heights every year as they grew. To anyone else, it would have been a worthless piece of splintered wood, headed for the dumpster—but not to her client, who wept when she realized what it was. (Total cost: $0.)

I sincerely believe that this kind of gift is the goal, especially given how much time real estate agents spend with clients, and the size of the transactions. But it may not be logistically possible for everyone to receive an experience that requires improvisation and bespoke, in-the-moment creation. Building a tool kit is a way to scale those extraordinary experiences, so that as many people as possible can experience these small, special touches.

If you're selling an apartment to a couple having a baby, get a pack of those protective plastic outlet covers and leave them in a drawer with a little note: "You've got big adventures coming up, so I took this off your to-do list." And because so many people move when they find out they're expecting, keep a case of those outlet covers in your office so you don't have to scramble. For newcomers to the area you specialize in, put together a guidebook of all your favorite spots—the best stroll, the best rigorous hike, the best apple cider donut. Print a dozen at a time.

Another agent I spoke with mentioned she'd sold eight pied-à-terres to suburban empty nesters in a single year. Do those people want yet another basic bottle of sparkling wine, available at every corner liquor store? Or would they prefer a behind-the-scenes tour of the art restoration facilities at the Met? Or tickets to the Village Vanguard? Or a membership to an art house movie theater in Brooklyn?

And if you can't or don't want to go that far, then take a minute to focus on making your back-pocket gift more thoughtful. Leave a Chemex coffeepot, with a box of filters and a bag of locally roasted ground coffee—because that's what people really need on their first morning in a new house before they've found the moving box with the espresso machine in it. I guarantee they'll think of you and your thoughtfulness every time they use it.

Fine, you're thinking, *except that restaurants and real estate are filled with opportunities, unlike my business.* I don't buy it. There are inflection points—patterns—in every business. Look closely, and you'll find them. And when you do, make sure you do something about it.

Another example: People tend to buy cars at specific points in their lives. Maybe they're starting a family and need a bigger vehicle, or their teenager has gotten a license and they're buying their child their first car. Or the kids are off to college, and it's time to get something a little sportier than the beat-up family boat they've been using to go back and forth from ballet and soccer practice.

If you know that people are going to come in, looking to buy a car for their teenager, why wouldn't you be prepared with an act of hospitality that will strengthen their connection to your brand? How would *you* feel about a car salesperson who pulled you aside and said, "Look, I know what it's like to have a newly licensed teenager on the road, so I got Frankie a year of Triple A. That way you know she's not going to get stranded out there."

A Triple A membership costs $119 at the time of this writing—a hundred and nineteen dollars that pretty much guarantees those parents will never buy a car from anyone else.

Or can you imagine the look a harried dad, struggling to install a booster seat, would give you if you sent him off your lot with a bag of Pepperidge Farm Goldfish, so his toddler doesn't get hangry on the way home—and a little DustBuster vacuum, so Dad can vacuum up all those orange crumbs and keep his brand-new car looking brand-new?

When people have the resources and the autonomy to imbue these transactions with their own thoughtfulness, salespeople become product designers. That car didn't come outfitted with a DustBuster, but that salesperson decided that for this specific customer, it would be better if it did. And they are going to feel a sense of pride in selling a product that they helped create.

And you should always—*always*—be on the lookout for the Legend. Let's say a guy has come back to your dealership every couple of years for a new car, and you've gotten to know him well. When his kids go off to college, he starts looking at vans; with a little more time on his hands, he's rediscovered his adolescent passion for surfing.

Why wouldn't you have a freshly waxed board waiting for him in the roof rack when he comes to pick up his new car? Obviously, this is a big gift, but it's also one with the potential to turn a faithful customer into a lifelong relationship. And if a surfboard's outside your budget, a can of surf wax on the dash with a bow and a note will do much the same thing.

Gifts, to me, are deeply meaningful, which is why I get so mad when a business gives me a cheap tote with a branded USB drive. Try harder! Do better! Gifts are a way to tell people you saw, heard, and recognized them—that you cared enough to listen, and to do something with what you heard. A gift transforms an interaction, taking it from transactional to relational; there is no better way than a gift to demonstrate that someone is more than a customer or a line item on a spreadsheet. And the right one can help you to extend your hospitality all the way into someone's life.

CHAPTER 19

SCALING A CULTURE

BACK IN THE DAY, the best restaurants in the world were in hotels. César Ritz ran the Hotel Splendide in Paris in the 1870s and introduced the robber barons of America to European luxury. In Monte Carlo, he met a French chef called Auguste Escoffier, and the rest is hospitality history—the two men's partnership ensured that, for the rest of the nineteenth century and all of the twentieth, the world's great hotels would be known for their restaurants.

Unfortunately, over time, the concept of the luxurious hotel restaurant fell out of favor. The restaurant in a hotel had become a sad add-on, the kind of grim spot you'd choose only if you were too exhausted from travel and meetings to leave the building. And if a new hotel did happen to attract a good restaurant, management would use separate entrances and branding to ensure the two felt distinct.

Early in 2010, Daniel and I were approached by Andrew Zobler, one of the partners in the hotel group that had developed and opened the Ace Hotel on Twenty-Ninth and Broadway. The Ace chain, with their affordable rooms, industrial and reclaimed aesthetic, and scene-heavy lobbies that doubled as workspaces had been runaway hits. Now Andrew wanted to talk to us about doing the food and beverage at a hotel with a new, higher-end concept: the rebirth of the Grand Hotel. It would be called the NoMad.

Andrew had the crazy idea to make the restaurant an integral part of the hotel once again—to bring back the days of Escoffier and Ritz. Both Daniel and I fell in love with the idea immediately, and we knew Andrew was the right person to do it with. We loved the way his other projects combined art, design, and retail alongside the food and beverage programs. We also saw an opportunity to rejuvenate a New York neighborhood that could use a little love.

The new site was mere blocks away from Eleven Madison Park, but the neighborhood was a throwback to the bad old days of the seventies: it was not unusual to witness a drug deal taking place in broad daylight. Broadway was lined with wholesale shops selling cheap trinkets, and the subway grates were covered by tarps with handles at the corner, so vendors could hide the knockoff bags they were selling when a cop drove by.

A hotel that didn't charge by the hour would play a major role in reinventing the neighborhood, and that was a powerful incentive for us. So was the management contract they were offering us: we wouldn't have to invest any money, which was good because we didn't have any.

Then came the hard part—talking to Danny Meyer.

Nobody Knows What They're Doing Before They Do It

"We have huge aspirations for Eleven Madison Park, and they're within reach," we told Danny. "At the same time, we don't want to be employees forever. We'd love to be owners of our own thing at the NoMad and continue working for you at Eleven Madison Park."

Danny asked to think about it for a while—and then he said no. "I can't be partners with you at one restaurant and competitors with you at another just a few blocks away."

There was some back and forth, and then he came back with an alternative: "How about you buy EMP from me?"

This was the last thing we'd expected to come out of that meeting. Still, almost without thinking, I said, "We'd love to."

I had no idea how we were going to pull it off. Looking back, I didn't even know what or how much I didn't know. But the biggest, scariest, most impossible-seeming accomplishments start with a simple commitment to do them.

I say this whenever someone shares their fears with me about taking a leap forward: **Nobody knows what they're doing before they do it.** When you're trying to level up, it's easy to psych yourself out by focusing on everything you don't know. But you've got to have faith in your ability to figure it out. A black diamond is scary if you usually ski blues. But you'll never advance if you always turn around to find an easier trail; eventually, you have to put your poles in the snow and push. Growth happens outside of your comfort zone. Whether on your ass or on your skis, don't worry—you will get down the hill, and you'll learn a lot along the way. (This is also why promoting people before they are ready works so well.)

Danny's offer came with a wise caveat: "You need to figure out if you can raise the money and buy the restaurant by February or March. No matter how hard we try to keep this under wraps, the secret will get out, and it'll be devastating for morale if the restaurant is in limbo for too long."

He was right, but it left us less than three months to raise a huge amount of money. And I don't mind telling you the experience was positively harrowing.

I started sitting down in the dining room with regulars. I didn't want to sound gauche by asking them for money, so I'd say, "Off the record, we've been given an opportunity to buy the restaurant. Do you know anyone who might want to invest?" Of course, I was hoping they'd be interested themselves, and a few of them were, so I spent a lot of time having drinks. But those were all dead ends—turns out, the kind of person who can afford to eat at an expensive restaurant can't necessarily afford to buy one.

Then Ernesto Cruz, a regular who worked upstairs in our building, said, "I help people buy and sell companies all the time. I'd be happy to help you." I thought: *I don't need help; I need money.* So I wasted another two or three weeks. Then one night after service, feeling desperate, I emailed Ernesto: "If your offer still stands, I could use some help."

Ernesto became my guardian angel. He put together a team of his colleagues who all worked pro bono to help usher me through the process. They showed me how to put together a deck, what modeling was, and how to demonstrate a return on investment. They set aside time so I could rehearse my pitch and give me feedback on my delivery. Then they came up with a list of potential investors, and I took my suit and my briefcase to Boston, to Chicago—even to Beverly Hills.

Asking for money is hard; it's humiliating to try to convince people that you're good enough for them to invest in. But I believed in Eleven Madison Park.

Ultimately, they introduced us to an investor named Noam Gottesman. We met him over lunch at Sushi Yasuda and got to know one another as individuals before talking about our ambitions for the restaurant. He must have seen something in us, because two weeks before the deadline was set to expire, we had the money. I'll forever be grateful for his vision and support.

At virtually the same time, we signed the deal to open the restaurant at the NoMad, which was set to open in March 2012. So, on November 11, 2011 (11/11/11), we announced to the staff that we had bought the restaurant. In a particularly dramatic turn of events, in that same week, *Eleven Madison Park: The Cookbook* came out, and we became the first restaurant in history to be elevated from one to three Michelin stars in a single year.

Make It Nice

We called our new company Make It Nice, after Daniel's signature phrase, back when his English was less refined. It had quickly become shorthand within the restaurant for "Pay a little extra attention to this"—whether "this" was a table of friends, or a dish, or even a side-work project. By that point, expectations were so clear, a team member could say, "Make it nice," to one of their colleagues, and without any further explanation, they would.

The symmetry of the words themselves appealed, reinforcing that this was a restaurant run by both sides of the wall. The kitchen "makes" food; in the dining room, we were "nice." (We were so adamant about breaking down the walls that divided us that—as you may have noticed—we didn't even use the common terms "back of house" and "front of house." Instead, we always referred to them as "the kitchen" and "the dining room.") Plus, "make" and "nice" had the same number of letters.

It was the perfect name for our company, encompassing both excellence and hospitality.

Creativity Is a Practice

The list of words we'd come up with because of a throwaway reference to Miles Davis in that early review of EMP had shaped the way we'd grown.

So when we signed the deal to open the NoMad, we knew we wanted to find another musical influence to serve as our muse.

If EMP was Miles Davis, then the NoMad would be the Rolling Stones.

The Rolling Stones are sex and drugs and Mick Jagger's dangerous energy strutting across the stage, right? But when the Stones were coming up, they bought and memorized every album they could find by American blues artists. They learned everything they could about the music they loved before imposing their own take. So yes, the Stones were loose—but in an incredibly studied and intentional way. *That* was how they'd reinvented rhythm and blues.

The NoMad was positioned at the intersection of uptown and downtown. We wanted to create an urban playground that could straddle both worlds and deliver the best of each. The place would be lush and luxurious but also democratic and awesome and easy and connective and loud and vibrant and loose and alive. And we were going to be as intentional in designing it as the Stones had been when they were studying the blues.

Once again, we were creating a place we'd want to go. Which meant an à la carte menu of technically perfect food and an exceptional, deep wine list, served by a young, high-energy staff in a fantastic New York space with a great playlist, played loud. If Eleven Madison Park was the place we'd choose to celebrate a special occasion (or when the dinner *was* the special occasion), the NoMad was where we'd go when it was time for an incredible night out.

For Daniel and me as businesspeople, and for us as a company, opening the NoMad was a huge leap forward, and came with all the challenges that haunt businesses during periods of growth and expansion. We got some stuff wrong, but we did a lot right—in large part because we went to great lengths to bring over the culture of hospitality we'd created at Eleven Madison Park.

It's impossible to overestimate how important it was for our new company for us to get the NoMad right. Plenty of bands have one hit, but if your sophomore album is a flop, you're a one-hit wonder. We wanted to be the Beatles, Nirvana, the Rolling Stones—evergreen, not poor Gary Wright of "Dream Weaver" fame. And in New York City, the paper of record plays an outsize role in determining which category you'll fall into, so nothing was more crucial than making sure the first review of the NoMad in *The New York Times* was a good one.

The pressure was intense.

To help focus and filter our ideas, I created a fictional character—a hedonistic, fifty-three-year-old gourmand and music lover, living and breaking hearts in the South of France—so we could design the public spaces of the NoMad as if they were rooms in his private home. We then held focused meetings to brainstorm all the elements that would make the place unique. Invariably, in every new group, someone would say, "I'm just not creative." Which would lead to my pulling them aside later to explain: that's not how creativity works.

To paraphrase the marketing guru Seth Godin, creativity is a practice. Even great creative minds like Sir Paul McCartney, Godin explains, have a system to help them be creative, to hone their ideas. In McCartney's case, time pressure, a regular schedule, and being comfortable with using a less-than-perfect word or musical phrase until he came up with a better one were all necessary for him to get to songs that are still beloved, fifty years later. Your practice may be different—and none of us is Paul McCartney—but it's time we dispel the myth that creativity must be spontaneous and is limited to geniuses. **Creativity is an active process, not a passive one.**

When we were designing the NoMad, the meetings we held were structured but also collaborative and exploratory. We were disciplined and intentional about creating a space where we could dream freely, which meant leaving every other concern at the door so we could give ourselves over to the process. In those rooms, it was safe to chase a seemingly silly idea that might just flower into a great one. There were no bad ideas (at least not at first), and no shame in presenting the earliest, half-formed kernel of one in the hopes that someone else might complete the thought—or use it as a springboard to something better. Even the Beatles were constantly contributing to one another's songs.

Once again, we were harnessing the collective brilliance of the team, playing off one another so effectively that in many cases, when I was later asked, "Whose idea was that?" I honestly didn't know.

Maya Angelou famously said, "You can't use up creativity. The more you use, the more you have." The more space we gave ourselves to dream, and the more trust we gave one another, the better we got.

On the nights we spent hours debating how the now-famous chicken for two would be served, I was grateful that my experience at EMP had helped me to reframe my fanatical attention to detail as a superpower. (We presented the whole bird on a copper platter, carved the breast, and served a fricassee of the dark meat on another plate, family-style.)

And since the NoMad would be open for breakfast, I spent an unreasonable amount of time searching for the perfect coffeepot. And every minute was worth it when I found the perfect one, a nod to the triangular Turkish *cezve*, made by Mauviel, the French copper cookware specialists.

It was clear to me right from the beginning that the library bar was going to be the beating heart of the hotel, so I oversaw every aspect of its design and execution. I drove a U-Haul to the massive Brimfield Antique Flea Market so I could handpick every chair before redoing them in the NoMad fabrics. And while it's common to purchase used books by the yard for a decorative library, there was no way we were going to fill our shelves with a generic jumble of old law textbooks and forgotten novels. In this, as with everything, we had to find our follow-through. So we asked our book curator to select books as if they were for our fictional character's library, which is how we ended up with sections on New York history, food and wine, music—and the occult. As Walt Disney said, people can feel perfection.

In the spirit of surprise and delight, we hid flasks of whiskey in hollowed volumes scattered throughout. If you found one of these real-life Easter eggs, it was yours to enjoy.

Jump-start the Culture

The majority of the opening management team at the NoMad came from Eleven Madison Park. That was deliberate. Because our plan had been to bring seasoned people to the new restaurant, we started staffing up at Eleven Madison Park a few months before.

I thought of those transplants from EMP as sourdough starter: not only would we have the benefit of their impeccable technical training, but they'd seed the new spot with our culture. They'd communicate, through words and their actions, everything that we stood for and believed in. Their passion and knowledge and all the values they'd accrued by watching the seasons pass from within the walls of Eleven Madison Park would infect everyone else we hired.

As you grow, you can't lose the very thing that gave you the opportunity to grow. When you consider expanding, in any form, you have to first stop and identify what makes your culture unique and decide in advance to protect whatever that is.

For us, that was our culture of Unreasonable Hospitality—going above and beyond, doing more, always giving our guests more than they expected. And a culture depends on the people who bring it to life every day; if we got that part right, the other pieces would fall into place.

The only major hire we made from outside the company was the general manager, Jeff Tascarella.

There were good reasons for us to make an exception in his case. Jeff had already been a general manager, and I wanted someone who'd been a boss before; he also had experience running a hotel restaurant, which I most certainly did not. Because the NoMad would be a little louder and looser than Eleven Madison Park, we needed someone with experience at a high-volume restaurant celebrated for its quality, and Jeff had run Scarpetta, a bustling, beloved, and excellent three-star restaurant in the Meatpacking District. Lastly, we wanted the NoMad to be cool—and Jeff was one of the coolest guys I knew.

Jeff became a huge part of the NoMad's success. Still, it's a measure of how important I thought it was to foster our culture by promoting from within that this was one of the only times in my tenure at the company that we ever hired a general manager from outside.

We took training very seriously in the run-up to opening the NoMad. Our budget for education was outrageous, according to the conventional wisdom, but I was betting the enormous amounts of time and energy and money we were spending would turn out to be a good investment. I'm always surprised when people spend a fortune on a new project, then skimp on training the people charged with bringing that project to life— a perfect example of what it means to be "penny-wise, pound-foolish."

By the time the doors opened, the hundred and fifty people on our dining room team had been alternating between classroom trainings and practical stages on the floor for weeks. They knew every wine by the glass, every dish, every service point. More important, they'd gotten a significant dose of our culture, and right from the source—either from me or from EMP's senior leadership.

Even EMP team members who hadn't come over to the NoMad had a hand in these trainings. Prior to the opening, we printed out hundreds of pages of notes from the pre-meal speeches I'd given over the past three years and asked the captains and managers at Eleven Madison Park to pick out concepts that had resonated the most with them—and the ones that had *stuck*, the ones that had made the most lasting impression, on them and on the team as a whole.

Compiling those ideas into a book forced us to put words to what we stood for. The experience was so positive I now think every company, no matter the size, should spend a few weeks hashing out every one of their core values and committing them to paper.

At the beginning, the Field Manual took the form of bound photocopies, but a couple of years later, we hired a designer and had a little red book printed, which would allow us to welcome our new employees with the same warmth and energy that we welcomed our guests.

Marry Up

It was review season again.

The next six months passed in a blur until the night we saw Pete Wells, the *New York Times* food critic who had taken over from Frank Bruni, walk into the NoMad's dining room.

The review gauntlet was no less stressful than previous ones had been. It was impossible to forget that the stakes were brutally high, but we put everything we had into it and applied every lesson we'd learned along the way. Thankfully, the process was short; just a few weeks later, in June 2012, the NoMad got three stars from *The New York Times*.

The review was titled "A Stellar Band Rearranges Its Hits." In it, Wells noted that we could have taken a more predictable and familiar route instead of the one we chose, which he said was "something rather novel and wonderful." As many great reviews as we'd gotten at Eleven Madison Park, I never openly wept reading one like I did that night.

Those tears were a combination of joy, relief, and pride. Our progress at EMP had been gradual; we'd steered an existing restaurant into becoming another kind of restaurant, and the marginal gains we'd made had been so incremental they felt inevitable.

The NoMad was different; we'd conceived it from the ground up. To make it happen, we'd taken a culture that we had evolved slowly and organically at EMP and imposed it on a completely new operation.

Obviously, a huge celebration with our team was in the cards that night. But Chef Magnus Nilsson of Sweden's Fäviken, a friend we'd made at that first, humiliating 50 Best, was doing a cookbook event at a rooftop garden called the Brooklyn Grange. So we went out quickly, to welcome him to New York.

This detour is only worth mentioning because it was the first time I met Christina Tosi, who was arriving just as I was leaving.

Though we'd never met, I'd had a crush on her for years. She was the pastry chef and owner of Milk Bar, celebrated around the world for Cereal Milk soft serve and Compost Cookies and her creative, nostalgic, irreverent approach to dessert. I knew she'd taken a postage-stamp-size storefront next to Momufuku Ssäm Bar and built it into one of the most beloved brands in the country; I also knew she was one of the most beautiful women I'd ever seen. And that night, with the three-star *New York Times* review under my arm and a little swagger to spare as a result, I walked right up to her and introduced myself.

We talked for only a minute—which was still long enough for me to get a glimpse of how generous, brilliant, and hilariously funny she was. She knew who I was, too, though after we were married, she admitted she'd been a little surprised to discover that the guy behind Eleven Madison Park was a normal person, not some stuck-up fancy-pants.

Then I got into a cab and headed back to the hotel to toast my team. It was a good night.

If it's not clear, the lesson here is this: Marry someone better than you. My partnership with Daniel made me a better restaurateur. My partnership with Christina has made me a better leader and better man.

Leaders Say Sorry

In spite of all the thoughtfulness we put into translating and preserving our culture, in those first months the NoMad was open I made one of the biggest mistakes of my career.

When we agreed to do the NoMad, I looked at my team at Eleven Madison Park and didn't see anyone ready to replace me as general manager. I had no desire to hire from outside; we believed too strongly in our culture of promoting from within. But since there wasn't anyone ready to do the job, I decided I would still act as GM at Eleven Madison Park while simultaneously opening the NoMad.

Can you guess how this ends?

If you've ever launched a new business, you know there aren't enough hours in the day. For months, I was at the NoMad pretty much every minute I was awake (and, since it was a hotel, quite a few non-waking ones, too).

Eleven Madison Park was only a few blocks away, but the restaurant was easy to neglect because the team in place had been there a long time and were operating at the highest level. In fact, that year, we'd moved up to number twenty-four on the 50 Best list—proof that the restaurant was running beautifully and the emphasis we'd put on hospitality was succeeding with our guests. However, even the most flawless and collaborative organization needs a boss.

Discussion and input are wonderful, but somebody needs to be on site to make decisions. If there's nobody to make the call, problems pile up: forward progress stalls completely, or random people step into the breach, take responsibility for a decision, and then face resentment from their peers—"Who died and made *you* president?" I'd left the restaurant in limbo, and morale was suffering.

Thankfully, there were people close enough to me to tell me the truth. I had a number of conversations with senior staff, who told me there was ambiguity where there shouldn't have been any: "Nobody's making decisions, and when someone does step up, they're accused of making a power grab. You have to name a GM, Will."

But all I heard was: *You need to work harder. You're not here and you need to be, so you better figure out a way to shoehorn an extra hour into the day so you can do your new job and this one, too.* No matter how guilty I felt, I was able to rationalize it away. "How bad could it be, when our guests were so happy?"

What I didn't understand was that a solid culture can stand up to some degree of abuse before the wear begins to show. Even if morale slips significantly, the guests won't feel it right away. Our team had a lot of love for EMP, and they took enormous personal and professional pride in providing spectacular hospitality. They were compartmentalizing, and doing a good job of it. But with enough drips, even the hardest rock is subject to erosion over time.

Finally, a longtime captain named Sheryl Heefner asked for a meeting with me. Sheryl was one of the best people on the team and one of my ride-or-dies—I trusted her implicitly.

The approach she took with me was effective precisely because she didn't tell me I was falling short. Instead, she held up a mirror, so I could see for myself where I'd gone wrong. And while Sheryl wasn't ordinarily an emotional person, she did get upset describing the damage I was doing to the restaurant by refusing to name a successor. I remember her asking, "Do you honestly not believe that a single person on our team is up to the task? You tell us there's nothing more important than being able to trust one another—but how are we supposed to believe that, when you won't trust anyone but yourself to do this job?"

There's nothing more devastating than a parent saying, "I'm not mad;

I'm disappointed." That was what Sheryl was saying, and I heard it. And as much as her words stung, you better believe I thanked her for coming to me.

My dad says, "Keep your eyes peeled," which means: listen, look, notice, learn; make sure you're not tumbling through life. Most important: Be aware when an item of real import is put in front of you.

That meeting with Sheryl was one of those moments. We were at a totally pivotal moment as a company, and I was screwing it up. I'd spent years telling people not to make themselves irreplaceable because that meant we couldn't promote them, but I hadn't had the wherewithal to see when my own role needed to change.

Worse, I'd betrayed one of our company's most closely held values. After screaming from the mountaintops about the importance of trusting the team, when it came time for me to walk the walk, I took a seat.

I knew immediately what I had to do—it was what I should have done the moment we signed the deal to make the NoMad a reality. I called a meeting with Kirk Kelewae, who had taken ownership of the beer program years before. He'd worked his way up from kitchen server to manager, and that day, I promoted him to GM.

After my private meeting with Kirk, I called an all-staff meeting and apologized to everyone in the room.

"This is the first time I've grown a company," I told them, "and this isn't the last mistake I'm going to make. But this was a big one." I had withheld the trust I'd been after them for years to show one another, and I'd damaged the culture we'd worked so hard to grow as a result. After I apologized, I announced that Kirk would be their new GM.

There were people in the room who probably would have preferred I'd said their name, but a decision had been made, and that made all the difference. The tension that had been growing vanished like the air from a popped balloon.

There is such power when a leader can admit to their mistakes and apologize for them. The idea that you're not going to make any errors is criminally stupid—as is the idea that if you don't own up to an error, nobody will notice you've made one. As hard as it is to hold yourself accountable publicly, it strengthens the bond between you and your team, because if you're willing to stand up and criticize yourself, people will always be more willing to receive criticism from you. The experience was a beautiful example of the power of vulnerability and its importance in leadership.

I hadn't trusted anyone else to be the general manager of EMP because I didn't think anyone would do the job as well as I was doing it—and, in fairness, I was probably right. Kirk *wasn't* ready to be a general manager yet, just as I hadn't been ready to be a general manager when I was given the same job at MoMA. (Apparently, I wasn't ready to be an owner, either.) **Sometimes the best time to promote people is before they are ready.** So long as they are hungry, they will work even harder to prove that you made the right decision.

Kirk grew into the job, just as he'd grown into running the beer program and every other position he'd held with us. And it was hugely meaningful for everyone else who worked there to see that the team was run by a guy who'd started out as a kitchen server. We'd said there were no limits, and we'd meant it. Now everyone could see that it was true.

No Guest Left Behind

The NoMad was a hit, right out of the gate.

Whatever the question was, the NoMad was the answer. We had breakfast regulars, lunch regulars, dinner regulars, late-night cocktail bar regulars—some days, those were the same people. It was exactly how we'd hoped people would use the different spaces we'd created. And the NoMad gave our company another gift, one that we hadn't foreseen.

As EMP continued climbing up the 50 Best list, our menu had become more complex, more involved, and more intricate, and our presentations had become more theatrical. A meal with us was increasingly lengthy, extensive, over-the-top—a production. With these changes, it had become difficult for our regulars; how many times a week can someone have a four-hour-long meal?

But with the NoMad just down the way, we could take the next step at EMP without deserting those beloved regulars; the NoMad gave them somewhere to go more regularly. Many of the dishes on the NoMad's menu had once been EMP's greatest hits, and there would be lots of familiar faces there; the attention to service would be recognizable, if slightly less dressed-up. The hotel's flexibility and relative informality meant that you could both schedule a breakfast meeting there and close out a great night with one last drink. And EMP would always be there for them on those nights when only a total luxury blowout dinner would do.

Sometimes, you outgrow your regulars; that's inevitable for any evolving organization. But we didn't want to fire ours; we wanted to keep them as part of our family. If you call your team your family, you need to invest in them and give them opportunities to grow with you and your organization, and you should extend the same courtesy to your most valued customers. Instead of cannibalizing our brand, the NoMad extended it.

Meanwhile, back at EMP, there was no longer anything holding us back . . . or so we thought.

CHAPTER 20

BACK TO BASICS

Throughout the years that we were climbing through the ranks of the 50 Best list, Daniel and I were traveling to food and wine conferences and culinary events all over the world. And any time we went to a new city, we'd take a night to go see what our competition was up to.

We found ourselves deeply inspired by every one of the restaurants on the list. At Narisawa in Japan, while we enjoyed our hors d'oeuvres, proofed bread dough baked tableside in a screaming-hot stoneware bowl, showcasing an ancient and elemental process that usually took place behind the scenes. It became one of the most delicious bites of our meal.

At Fäviken in Sweden, instead of twenty servers describing twenty different dishes to twenty different tables, our friend Magnus came out from the kitchen, clapped his hands, and announced the next course, which everyone in the dining room then ate at the same time, like guests at a dinner party in his home.

At Mugaritz in Spain, we pounded spices and seeds for soup in an iron bowl with a pestle. Then a captain invited us to run the pestle around the edge as if it were a Tibetan singing bowl, and for a breathtakingly beautiful moment, the entire dining room came together in community to create music.

At Alinea in Chicago, pastry chefs brought ingredients for dessert into the dining room, artfully scattering chocolate, custards, pralines, pieces of cake, and fresh berries across a silicone tablecloth—Kandinsky, if his medium had been sugar. Everyone else on earth looked at a table and saw a table; Chef Grant Achatz looked at a table and saw a plate.

These crescendos were both thoughtful and beautiful. They provided these already extraordinary meals with an exclamation point within the experience, an unforgettable moment that was as delicious to recount weeks later as it had been to eat.

And they reinforced why the 50 Best list had been so good for our industry. The best restaurants in the world were encouraging and inspiring one another to ever-greater heights when they might instead have become complacent. The friendly competition and exchange of ideas pushed the whole profession forward.

We felt confident in the crescendos we'd added to the experience of dining at EMP; what was missing now was a sense of place. It was the age of Noma, and every one of the restaurants at the top of the list was serving an experience that was so deeply specific to where they were, the meal wouldn't make sense anywhere else. This felt especially important in an increasingly globalized and homogenous world where you could travel sixteen hours on a plane, then walk down a luxury row virtually identical to the one in the city you'd left behind.

Plus, we saw a real opportunity. *Our* restaurant was in New York— not only the birthplace of so much art and music and industry (and so many food traditions), but an important and underrecognized agricultural area. And while each of the best fine-dining restaurants in New York did have a strong sense of place, the places they were celebrating *weren't* New York, but Japan, and Italy, and France. So when EMP made it to number ten on the 50 Best list in 2012, we were resolved to explore what it meant to be a restaurant of, from, and about New York.

We threw ourselves into research and turned up such a wealth of inspiration that we abandoned our new menu format (and, with it, the diner's ability to choose what they would eat). We adopted a straight tasting menu with a New York theme, to ensure that everyone who ate with us would experience all the things *we* were excited about.

The meal began with a savory take on the iconic black-and-white cookie and ended with chocolate-covered pretzels. There was sturgeon smoked at the table under a glass dome. We learned that the potato chip had been invented in New York, so we made our own and had custom chip bags printed, so expensive I practically had to hide the bill from myself. (Hey, 95/5.)

Tartare has roots in New York City, so we used New York carrots—grown in the nutrient-rich mud that upstate farmers call "black muck"—to make carrot tartare. And instead of leaving a bottle of cognac on the table at the end of the meal, our gift was a custom-labeled applejack from Laird's, the first licensed distillery in the area, dating back to 1780.

Our cheese course became a Central Park picnic. We commissioned Ithaca Beer Company to make a Picnic Ale, made pretzels with that beer, and partnered with the iconic New York store Murray's Cheese to make a cheese washed in it. The course was served in picnic baskets made in upstate New York, on porcelain plates that looked like paper made by a Brooklyn artist named Virginia Sin.

Like many a wide-eyed tourist, I'd been fleeced by a three-card-monte dealer in Times Square when I was a kid coming in from Westchester to meet my dad at work. I wanted to incorporate a little of that old-school grittiness and some sleight of hand into the experience of dining with us—which led to my meeting with a team of magicians to create a trick where you picked the main ingredient in your dessert by choosing a card, though a chocolate flavored with that ingredient was already secretly on the table. (A sweeter ending than losing your allowance to a con man, for sure.)

An aside: the experience of coming up with the magic trick was fascinating. I had reached out to a company called theory11 because I wanted them to make us a custom deck of cards. But the owner, Jonathan Bayme, showed up for our first meeting with the magician Dan White, so I wasn't surprised when he suggested a magic trick instead.

I was immediately intrigued. I'd talked so much to the team about our responsibility to create magic in a world that needs more of it that the chance to approach this literally was too good not to consider. Especially when, after a couple of hours of brainstorming, Dan White blew my mind by describing the trick we ended up using.

My jaw dropped. "That's incredible! But how would we do it?"

Dan shook his head. "Oh, I have no idea. We'll have to figure it out."

I loved that—how unfazed he was to not know and how confident he was that we'd figure it out.

Too many people approach creative brainstorming by taking what's practical into consideration way too early in the process. Working with Jonathan and Dan reinforced what I'd always believed: **Start with what you want to achieve, instead of limiting yourself to what's realistic or sustainable.** Or, as I like to say, don't ruin a story with the facts. Eventually, you'll reverse engineer your great idea and figure out what's possible and cost-effective and all the other boring grown-up stuff. But you should start with what you want to achieve.

(When Dan heard the title of this book, he shared this wildly appropriate quote from Teller, the silent half of the famed magic duo Penn and Teller: "Sometimes magic is just someone spending more time on something than anyone else might reasonably expect.")

We also introduced a new, much longer mission statement for the team, complete with a New York City subway map–inspired graphic. This new statement included *everything* we were striving to embody: to be a New York restaurant, run equally by the kitchen and the dining room; to carry ourselves in a way that was genuine and good; to always be learning and leading; to balance the classic and the contemporary; to take risks in pursuit of reinvention; and to create a culture of family and fun. Finally, we made our goal four Michelin stars to match the number of leaves in our logo, even though Michelin didn't even give four stars!

When the new menu debuted, I wanted every table to understand the rich history and the wealth of stories behind every course on the new menu. Not wanting to leave any part to chance or discretion, I wrote exactly what I wanted the captains to say, had them memorize it, and drilled them over and over and over again.

We introduced the new menu on a Tuesday in September 2012. Four days later, *The New York Times* food critic Pete Wells came in for lunch.

It was a shock to see him; usually, they give you a minute or two to settle in after a big change. But I was able to exhale when I saw he'd ended up in Natasha McIrvin's section. Natasha was, without question, one of our best captains—exceptionally talented, dedicated to excellence in all things, and unflappable even under intense pressure. I knew she'd get the story we were telling just right.

On his way out the door—I was trying to be unobtrusive, futzing around in a corner next to the bar—Pete Wells looked me right in the eyes and nodded. That was deeply unusual: the critic and the restaurateur never acknowledge each other. I took it as a sign that we'd crushed it.

So you can imagine my surprise when, just a few days later, the *Times* published the article he'd written—a scathing takedown titled "Talking All Around the Food: At the Reinvented Eleven Madison Park, the Words Fail the Dishes."

I'll spare you, but it included such descriptive gems as: "stilted," "bloat," and this knockout punch, my personal favorite: "By the end of the four hours, I felt as if I'd gone to a Seder hosted by Presbyterians." The article was so awful that in their own gleeful piece about it (that's right: it was so bad, there were schadenfreude-y think pieces written about how bad it was), *Eater* dubbed him "Pete 'The Punisher' Wells."

And he might as well have addressed it directly to me. He didn't love everything he ate, but he loved a lot of it. The problem was what he called "the speeches."

It was deeply humiliating. And there was nothing I was less excited for than to stand up and confess that my bad decisions had gotten us this savage review. In moments like this, in an effort to not look bad in front of their team, leaders tend to brush mistakes under the rug, foolishly hoping that everyone will forget they've happened. Instead, I once again stood up in pre-meal to take responsibility and apologize.

There was a little bit of good news, though. The piece wasn't a true review with stars, which might have devastated the business, but a "Critic's Notebook"—the critical equivalent of a warning shot. And it did exactly what it was intended to do: it allowed me to see the error of my ways and course-correct.

After some soul searching, I realized that in introducing the New York menu, I'd made two mistakes. One I don't regret making, though we fixed it anyway. The other I do.

The first mistake was going too far. (That's the one I don't regret.) Yes, part of that exuberance was a show-offy "Look what we can do!" But pushing the limits is also an unavoidable part of the creative process. If you don't explore the outer perimeter, how else will you know where the line is? A lot of those ideas were good; if we hadn't given ourselves the freedom to investigate them, we would never have known which of them to keep.

That mistake—trying to do too much—was easy to fix. We didn't change everything; we knew we couldn't be all things to all people. We kept the magic trick, because we could see, every night, that people loved it; it was a crescendo they'd still be talking about weeks, even years, later. But we did get rid of a lot of the speeches. And the potato chip course, which—painfully—meant recycling those expensive bags.

The second mistake I'd made was more serious. I'd wanted to make sure every idea we had was communicated properly, so I'd insisted the team learn a spiel. I'd made them performers, ruling out any possibility of a real, quality conversation between them and the guests. Of course the experience had felt inauthentic to Wells; there had been no room for Natasha to connect with him. I had taken away her ability to be herself at the table.

Not every guest wanted a history lesson during their dinner. Many were charmed and wanted to engage with us. But some people were there to talk to their companions or to eat; they wanted us to drop off their food and leave them alone. I had stripped the team of their authority to read the table and deliver an appropriate level of detail—to tailor the service experience to the guest. In my pursuit of a sense of place, I'd actually made the meal less hospitable.

Worse, it was essentially the same mistake I'd made the year before, when I'd hesitated to promote a general manager. Once again, the guy known for talking about how much he trusted his team had acted as if he didn't trust them at all.

In truth, I'm not surprised I made this mistake—and I'm almost certain I'll make it again in the future. My compulsive attention to detail is one of my superpowers; it's how I take aim at perfection. But that tendency also means I'm always walking a tightrope between my desire to guarantee excellence by controlling everything and knowing I want to create an environment of empowerment and collaboration and trust among the people who work for me. Like excellence and hospitality, these two qualities—control and trust—are not friends.

I like to think I gain awareness every time I make this mistake. I have surrounded myself with people I trust, who tell me when it's time to back off. But I'm pretty sure managing the tension between these two is an issue I will struggle with for the rest of my career. All I can do is stay aware, so my superpower doesn't turn into my villain origin story. And when I do (inevitably) screw up, I need to fix the mistake quickly and with as little ego as possible.

I returned to trusting people on the team to introduce the menu in the way they saw fit and to deliver an appropriate level of information for their tables.

Meanwhile, we kept inching up the 50 Best list. In 2013 (despite the Presbyterian Seder), we moved up to number five. In 2014, we were number four. And early in 2015, Pete Wells came back. By his second visit, we knew he was there to give us a proper re-review. No more warning shots.

It was nerve-racking to see him, because we'd stuck to our guns on a number of things he'd hated. But we'd used his criticism wisely; we'd changed what we wanted to change and were proud of the experience we were giving our guests.

In March of that year, he awarded us four stars. It was, as I like to say, the worst four-star review ever in the history of *The New York Times*. It still makes me laugh to read it. He's so grumpy! He can't resist calling back to his first experience with the New York menu in 2012, calling it "the most ridiculous meal I've ever had."

Then he proceeds to list fault after fault with the new experience—except that he's finally forced to cry uncle: "Objections . . . buzzed before my eyes so insistently that at times they blinded me to what was going on in the soaring Art Deco space across from Madison Square Park. Which was: a roomful of people almost goofy with happiness . . . and finally even me, the overthinking picker of nits and finder of faults. Under the restaurant's relentless, skillful campaign to spread joy, I gave in."

We did celebrate that night, though I should note that holding on to four stars feels very different than earning them for the first time; the mood was more relief than jubilation.

But in pre-meal the next day, I congratulated the team, acknowledging that the review was an affirmation of their commitment to Unreasonable Hospitality. Wells hadn't agreed with everything we were doing—he didn't even *like* a lot of it. And yet, by sticking to the principles of

Unreasonable Hospitality, we'd left him with no choice but to acknowledge that he loved the way we made people feel.

Serve What You Want to Receive

At the 50 Best in 2015, the air was thick with rumors, as always—and the big one was that we were going to come in at number one. It's best to ignore gossip, of course, but we're human and it's hard. So our hopes were up.

But the speculation was dead wrong: instead of going from four to one, we slid backward, from four to five.

It was a real blow. Of course, it's pretty incredible to be named one of the top five restaurants in the world, no matter where you land. But this was the first time since we'd gotten on the list that we had fallen backward. As hard as we were pushing, something wasn't working.

In retrospect, I think that slide backward was the best thing that could have happened to us, because it motivated us to change one last time. And we needed to change; the rumblings were already there.

Over the course of that year, Daniel and I had taken our usual field trips to the very best restaurants, and we had begun to notice another feature—or perhaps "bug" is a better word—that most of those spectacular meals had in common.

They were just *too much*.

As inspired as we were by those incredible crescendos, as wowed as we were by course after course of faultless food paired with remarkable wines, it was also overwhelming. Jaded as it might sound, we were starting to experience some fatigue. The excellence of the service and the theatricality of some courses were impressive; still, it was hard the next day to remember what exactly we'd eaten, or any part of the conversation we'd had while we were there. The truth was that 75 percent of the way through most of those meals, we were done and dusted—bellies full, restless, and ready to go. All this was in the back of our minds as we sat down to taste our own new menu at the end of 2015.

Daniel and I had dinner together at the restaurant every season, the day after the menu changed. This was mostly practical; you already know I believe it's vitally important for a leader to experience the service they're providing just as an ordinary customer would. An idea is often different in practice than it is in conception, and eating the menu as guests gave us the opportunity to make adjustments when, say, we discovered a presentation we'd been excited about felt too fussy, or when we were trying to be generous but ended up stuffing the guest past the point of pleasure.

Those dinners also provided a valuable quarterly check-in for Daniel and me, a more intentional opportunity to connect than the ten thousand quick texts and hurried kitchen hallway conversations that made up the majority of our daily interactions.

Indeed, that night we were not only analyzing our meal but had slipped into a deeper, more intense meaning-of-life-type conversation. Or were trying to, anyway—and I say trying because, as dialed-in as the service was, it felt like we were constantly being interrupted. With every distraction, I became increasingly annoyed; we ended up leaving before dessert was served and heading to an Irish pub a couple of blocks away so we could finish our conversation in peace.

When I got home that night, I did the math.

For every course, the table was set with fresh silverware, new wineglasses were placed, food was served and spieled, wine was poured. After we were done eating, the plates were cleared, and the table was crumbed. Those six actions happened for every single course—which meant that over a fifteen-course menu, we were being interrupted *ninety times* over the entirety of our meal. And that didn't even include the introduction to the menu or any mid-course check-in.

Ninety times—when our stated goal was to create an environment where people could connect over the table, where, as I had said a thousand times, the service and the food and the environment were mere ingredients in the recipe of human connection. That is unreasonable, but it's not hospitality.

We'd always believed we should serve what we wanted to receive. Serve only what you want to serve, and you're showing off. Serve only what you think other people want, and you're pandering. Serve what you genuinely want to receive, and there will be authenticity to the experience.

That was why the restaurant had changed so much over the years. Not because we had the words "endless reinvention" on the wall, but because *we'd* changed, and what we wanted to receive had as well. I was twenty-six years old when I took over the dining room at Eleven Madison Park and forty when Daniel and I parted ways. You change a lot between twenty-six and forty—and as you change, what you want to receive changes, too.

We were no longer serving what we wanted to receive.

Return to First Principles

A mission statement's role, in any organization, is to articulate the non-negotiables. It needs to be clear and simple and easily understood, so that any time you're making any decision, no matter how big or small, you can rely on it as a filter to decide. Will taking an action help you achieve the goal laid out in the mission statement? Or will it take you away from that goal? That way, the decision is already made for you—all you have to do is ask yourself the question.

The complicated mission statement we introduced with the New York menu contained everything we wanted to embody: our commitment to one another, our love of New York, our absurd ambitions, and our desire to take care of our guests. But it was too much.

Pete Wells had never seen that complicated, convoluted mission statement, but he'd felt it. No wonder he'd struggled to understand what the restaurant was! We hadn't known ourselves.

It was time to get back to basics. Daniel and his team made unbelievably delicious food; my dining room team was as good as any in the world at spreading joy through Unreasonable Hospitality. And so, in reaffirming our superpowers, we rediscovered our nonnegotiables, landing on a simple, elegant phrase I posted above the time clock so every one of us would see it, every day:

"To be the most delicious and gracious restaurant in the world."

We weren't going to stop being "of" New York or treating our colleagues like family. We weren't going to stop shooting for a fourth Michelin star, an ambition that could never be satisfied. But gracious and delicious—those were the criteria. Period.

As my dad says: "Don't run away from what you don't want; run *toward* what you do." We didn't make the changes we made over that year because we were running away from complexity or difficulty or ambition, but because we were running toward a purer experience.

Every change we'd ever made before had been additive. More intensity, more courses, more complexity, more components on the plate, more wines, more steps of service—more, more, more.

This time, we went in the other direction. We were proud of what we could do, but there was no need for all of it. Instead, we could distill what we were delivering down to what made us special: the recognition that all this excellence was in service of Unreasonable Hospitality.

The first and most radical change was cutting the menu in half, shortening it from fifteen to seven courses. Every one would be memorable—extraordinary. And even though we'd slashed the number of courses, we didn't cut a single person from the dining room staff. Instead, we doubled down, going from two Dreamweavers to four.

In the process of developing the New York menu, we'd moved away from the revised menu format and our core belief that the diner should have agency, the ability to choose. Why had we gotten rid of that, when it exemplified the kind of Unreasonable Hospitality we wanted to offer?

We would return to this concept of the meal as a dialogue. And finally, we were ready to do it the way we'd wanted to do it in the first place, the way they did it at Rao's. There would be no menu at all, just a conversation about what you wanted to eat and what you didn't.

That conversation was more than just conversation—it forged a connection. No more scripts. This was the beginning of a relationship.

Kirk had moved on to open a new restaurant for us, so Billy Peelle, who had left EMP to work at the NoMad, came back as general manager—the perfect person to usher in this new iteration. Billy took genuine pleasure in creating a warm environment for the people he worked with and remarkable experiences for our guests. He embodied Unreasonable Hospitality as much as anyone I'd ever worked with, and he led with authenticity and humility.

The day after we introduced the new menu, Daniel and I sat down and had dinner. And after a truly extraordinary three-hour-long meal, we felt, after all those iterations and all those years, that the restaurant had become what it was meant to be. By paring our vision down to its essentials, we had finally found ourselves. I truly believe, at that moment, we were finally operating as the best restaurant in the world.

Just a few months later, the 2016 50 Best awards were held in New York City for the first time. Since virtually everyone who votes for those awards attends the ceremony, there were suddenly a lot of them in our city, which meant we had the opportunity to host many of them at EMP. The changes we'd made had been so effective—the restaurant felt so good—that we weren't even nervous, just fired up to show the world who we were and what we stood for. We put our best foot forward, but mostly, we confidently and warmly welcomed our colleagues into our home. And it felt awesome.

That year at the awards, we were voted number three in the world. More important, we won the first-ever Art of Hospitality Award, reflecting the impact we were having on the industry.

Since 2002, the awards had only ever acknowledged chefs and their food. The introduction of a hospitality award was an indication the pendulum was swinging the other way, shining a light on the people in the dining room who worked tirelessly to provide fantastic service. It meant a lot to me personally that we won that inaugural award. Unreasonable Hospitality was no longer something that mattered only to us; it was starting to matter in our industry.

The Most Delicious and Gracious Restaurant in the World

The next year, we headed to the 50 Best awards in Melbourne.

On the day of the awards, I took a long walk with Christina, trying not to let my anxiety get the best of me, before heading back to the hotel to change into my tux. Gary Obligacion of Alinea tied my bow tie; I've never learned how.

As always, they started at fifty and counted down: forty, then thirty, then twenty. The further they got, the more excited and nervous we got; the longer we didn't hear our names, the better.

I pretty much blacked out when they got to number ten and only came to again when they hit number three. Still not us—so we had to be either number one or number two. Then they announced Osteria Francescana (owned by our friend Massimo, who'd ribbed us about our sad faces during that first, humiliating ceremony), and we knew we'd won it.

After seven years of hard work, creativity, a maniacal attention to detail, and a truly unreasonable dedication to hospitality, Eleven Madison Park was named the best restaurant in the world.

It was an incredible feeling, one of the best of my life. I kissed my wife, and Daniel and I went up to the stage with Billy Peelle and Dmitri Magi, our chef de cuisine. It was not lost on me, as I was handed the award, that I was the first dining room person ever to take part in accepting the award on behalf of their restaurant.

In my speech, I talked about the nobility of service, the importance of naming for ourselves that the work we do is important. This felt especially meaningful because everyone in that room had dedicated their careers to creating memorable experiences. Everyone there had helped people celebrate their most important moments and given them comfort when they needed an escape. All of us were creating magical worlds in a world that needed a little bit more magic.

I thanked our magnificent team (and asked them not to wreck the restaurant celebrating; we'd do that together when we got home). Not just the hundred and fifty people who worked for us at the time, but the countless others who, over the past eleven years, had given so much of themselves in pursuit of taking care of others. And I thanked Daniel for understanding that how we made our guests feel mattered as much as any one dish we served them.

The tribute provided me with a moment to reflect on how far we'd come, and everything that brought us there. At one level, it's fundamentally ridiculous to say one restaurant is the best in the world. But the award acknowledges the restaurant making the greatest impact on the industry at a given time, the one that is changing the conversation and charting a new course for everyone.

We'd won because all of us in the kitchen and the dining room came together to create an experience that was thoughtful, gracious, and really, really nice. We'd won because of our collective focus on Unreasonable Hospitality.

We had set out to achieve a seemingly impossible goal: to embody both excellence and hospitality—concepts in tension with each other, if not outright conflict. We had made the decision to be as joyfully unreasonable in our creative pursuit of hospitality in the dining room as the best restaurants all over the world already were in the kitchen. We'd decided not to reserve our best efforts only for what was on the plate, but to use everything at our disposal to make the people we worked with and the people we served feel seen and heard; to give them a sense of belonging and to create an environment where they could connect with others.

It was our pursuit of excellence that brought us to the table, but it was our pursuit of Unreasonable Hospitality that took us to the top.

EPILOGUE

WE ARRIVED HOME TRIUMPHANT: seven years of single-minded focus had turned a far-fetched goal, scrawled onto a cocktail napkin, into a reality.

It was time to start our next chapter.

For the first time, we made plans to do a complete renovation of the restaurant. There had been lots of physical changes to the room over the years, but we'd always been making tweaks to what still felt like Danny Meyer's restaurant. It was time for it to become completely, entirely ours.

The renovation meant we'd be closed for a few months. By then we knew that without our team, the restaurant was just four walls, some tables, and a stove. We couldn't afford to lose a single one of them, so we opened a whole new restaurant in the Hamptons—a more casual offshoot, which we called EMP Summer House, and moved the whole group out there with us. That project was both creatively satisfying and commercially successful, not to mention wildly fun.

We reopened Eleven Madison Park in the fall, serving the same streamlined experience we'd debuted the year before, in an elegant room designed exclusively for us. And for a while, everything was just right—until it wasn't.

People have spent a lot of time speculating about why Daniel and I decided to go our separate ways. The truth is simple: we fell out of love. People grow apart. You realize that you and your partner no longer share the same interests, the same priorities—you're no longer looking at the world in the same way. Nothing can rob you of what you've shared. But when it's over, it's over.

When Daniel and I realized that the best path forward was to separate, I asked my dad for advice, as I have done during all the difficult moments in my life. He told me, "This next year is going to be one of the most challenging of your life. You're going to be faced with countless difficult decisions. Every time you find yourself at a crossroads, I want you to ask yourself what 'right' looks like, then do that." Then he told me that this advice wasn't always going to be easy to follow because often doing what's "right" isn't always best for you in the short term.

Dividing the company was not simple. By then, we had NoMad Hotels in New York, Los Angeles, and Las Vegas and a fast-casual restaurant in New York called Made Nice. We had EMP Summer House in the Hamptons, EMP Winter House in Aspen, and were working on three brand-new projects: two in London, and one in New York. And, of course, there was still Eleven Madison Park.

We spent months trying to figure out how the split should work, but we weren't making much progress. Then one night, we hosted a fundraiser for an organization addressing food insecurity called Rethink Food, launched by one of our former colleagues.

The evening was a brilliant success; Neil Patrick Harris emceed, and we raised tons of money for a cause close to my heart. At the very end, after the food had been served and cleared, my friend Jon Batiste sat down behind the piano. I called everyone on the team who was still there out from the kitchen, and the whole crew and I stood in the doorway, watching Jon perform a magical, six-song acoustic set—the last of which was his devastatingly beautiful cover of the Louis Armstrong classic, "What a Wonderful World."

I got home late that night. Christina was out of town, so I poured myself a huge, shift-drink-size glass of red wine, and put the recorded version of that song on repeat. I listened to it about two dozen times and refilled my glass at least twice. By the third glass, it was crystal clear what "right" looked like.

In our desire to hold on to part of the company we'd spent the past fourteen years building, we were effectively ripping it apart. "Right" was allowing the company we'd built together to stay together. "Right"—as inconceivable, as impossible as it seemed—meant that one of us would have to walk away, from all of it.

A couple of months later, Daniel and I gathered the team together so I could say goodbye.

I loved Eleven Madison Park. But the Unreasonable Hospitality we'd delivered had nothing to do with the storied room or the chairs or the art or the kitchen or the address. The heart of the company was the team— the collection of individuals I'd surrounded myself with—and the work that we did together every single day, taking care of one another and the people we served. I'll always be proud of the traditions we established, all the wild ideas we brought to life, and the countless people we made happy. I also knew that I could do all of that again, using everything I'd learned at EMP and the principles we developed over the fourteen years I was there.

Letting go was hard. It's still hard! But I have found catharsis in writing this book—in reliving the journey and relearning the lessons. It has reinforced for me how much I love hospitality, both in service and in leadership.

The global pandemic hit just a few months after I left EMP, and I watched as some of my closest friends and colleagues struggled to keep their businesses alive. A phone call led a small group of us to launch the Independent Restaurant Coalition, which successfully lobbied for federal relief for independent restaurants across America. At a moment when I might otherwise have been sidelined, I was able to act as an advocate for the industry I love—including during a surreal trip to the White House.

And as if that wasn't enough to keep me busy, Christina and I also welcomed a new member to our family: our daughter Frankie, named after her extraordinary grandfather. I've spent a lot of the past year at my own kitchen table catering to the most significant VIP of my career, in a high chair for one.

As the world has begun to open back up, I find myself spending time with leaders from many different industries—from the medical field to luxury retail to real estate and beyond. All of them recognize the remarkable power of giving the people on their teams and their customers more than they expect, and every one of them has chosen to be unreasonable in that pursuit. All of them have made the decision to join the hospitality economy—and I hope you will, too.

I APPRECIATE YOU

Writing this book has been one of the great experiences of my life, and as I go through the final edits and work on these last pages I can't help but take a moment to pause and reflect about how appreciative I am for the many people who played such an important role in getting it over the line.

One of the reasons I chose to work in restaurants was because I don't like working alone; I always do my best work when I'm part of a team. And in Laura Tucker I found the best teammate I could have ever hoped for in writing this book. She helped me take all of the crazy ideas from my head and weave them together into the words on these pages. Her exceptional warmth, unbelievable talent, and endless patience proved to be exactly what I needed through this process. I'll be forever grateful for the many, many hours we spent together bringing this to life.

In Simon Sinek I found the best coach I could have ever asked for on this journey. We spent countless days together across a table going page by page through this book, looking for every opportunity to make it just a little bit better. He challenged me, inspired me, encouraged me, and pushed me to create something I would be proud of. His belief in me made me believe in myself.

Adrian Zackheim and Merry Sun at Penguin Random House were such incredible partners to me throughout this process. Their appreciation for what I had to say gave me the confidence to want to say it to the world.

I'll forever be grateful to David Black for being by my side and supporting me all of these years. He is one of the warmest and most caring people I know—and an absolute pit bull when he needs to be. It brings me so much joy to have him in my corner.

No one knows better than a restaurateur how many people, working tirelessly behind the scenes, it takes to bring an idea to life. I'm so thankful for the amazing hospitality that was extended to me by the amazing team at PRH and Optimism Press: Kirstin Berndt, Ellen Cipriano, Linda Friedner, Tara Gilbride, Jen Heuer, Katie Hurley, Brian Lemus, Andrea Monagle, Niki Papadopoulos, Jessica Regione, Mary Kate Skehan, Laila Soussi, Margot Stamas, Sara Toborowsky, and Veronica Velasco. Their passion for the craft and attention to detail was inspiring.

This book wouldn't exist without Danny Meyer, who gave me the foundation upon which I built all my ideas about service and leadership. He opened the doors for so many of my peers in the industry and showed us that the hospitality business is a truly noble profession.

Tom Clifton spent an extraordinary amount of time lending me his thoughtful perspectives, truly making this a better book, as did many other amazing people who were so generous over the last year reading and rereading this manuscript, all the while helping me to make sure it was the best version it could possibly be: Kevin Boehm, John Erickson, Seth Godin, Ben Leventhal, Roger Martin, and Jann Schwarz.

I am lucky to have friends and former colleagues who were so generous with their time as I navigated through the final steps of this process: Katy Foley and Kate Fraser for spreading the word about this book, and Juliette Cezzar for helping to make it beautiful.

I work with an exceptional team—Billy Peelle and Natasha McIrvin—who worked extra hard to keep our company running so that I could have the time and space to focus on this book. And I have found amazing partners and supporters in Michael Forman, Bill Helman, and Gaurav Kapadia. I'm thankful for their passion and dedication, and their belief in me. I am so excited for all that we are building together.

And I could not be more grateful for my beautiful family—my wife, Christina, and our daughter, Frankie—for breathing life into my life. . . . I love you blindly, unreasonably, and without end.

NOTES

40 **Former navy captain:** Simon Sinek, *Leaders Eat Last* (New York: Portfolio / Penguin, 2017).

125 **Frustrated, the Imagineers reminded:** Julianna Alley, interview by Simon Sinek, Disney Institute, Lake Buena Vista, FL, March 4, 2022.

130 **Thankfully, it was good:** Frank Bruni, "Two Upstarts Don Their Elders' Laurels," *The New York Times,* January 10, 2007, https://www.nytimes.com/2007/01/10/dining/reviews/10rest.html.

162 **In his review:** Frank Bruni, "Imagination, Say Hello to Discipline," *The New York Times*, December 9, 2008, https://www.nytimes.com/2008/12/10/dining/reviews/10rest.html.

178 **He described watching:** Frank Bruni, "A Daring Rise to the Top," *The New York Times*, August 11, 2009, https://www.nytimes.com/2009/08/12/dining/reviews/12rest.html.

178 **In writing about:** Frank Bruni, "Four Stars, More Thoughts," *The New York Times*, August 12, 2009, https://dinersjournal.blogs.nytimes.com/2009/08/12/four-stars-more-thoughts.

185 **But the engine:** Jay-Z, *Decoded* (New York: One World, 2010).

193 **As Oliver Strand wrote:** Oliver Strand, "At Eleven Madison Park, Fixing What Isn't Broke," *The New York Times*, September 7, 2010, https://www.nytimes.com/2010/09/08/dining/08humm.html.

228 **The review was titled:** Pete Wells, "A Stellar Band Rearranges Its Hits," *The New York Times*, June 19, 2012, https://www.nytimes.com/2012/06/20/dining/reviews/the-nomad-in-new-york.html.

239 **So you can imagine:** Pete Wells, "Talking All Around the Food: At the Reinvented Eleven Madison Park, the Words Fail the Dishes," *The New York Times*, September

17, 2012, https://www.nytimes.com/2012/09/19/dining/at-the-reinvented-eleven
-madison-park-the-words-fail-the-dishes.html.

242 **Which was: a roomful:** Pete Wells, "Restaurant Review: Eleven Madison Park in
Midtown South," *The New York Times*, March 17, 2015, https://www.nytimes
.com/2015/03/18/dining/restaurant-review-eleven-madison-park-in-midtown
-south.html.

INDEX